THE KEW GARDENER'S GUIDE TO

GROWING
PERENNIALS

THE KEW GARDENER'S GUIDE TO

GROWING
PERENNIALS

THE ART AND SCIENCE TO
GROW YOUR OWN PERENNIALS

RICHARD WILFORD

FRANCES
LINCOLN

Contents

Introduction to growing perennials

—

THE VALUE OF PERENNIALS

There is a huge variety of plants that can be called perennials, but the one thing they have in common is that they flower year after year. They will fill your garden with flowers and come back the next year to do it all again. Most die back for part of the year, usually winter, but they rise again, with fresh new leaves and a display of flowers that may last several weeks before they slowly fade away and retreat back to their roots.

Perennials are just one group of plants in a garden, along with trees, shrubs, bulbs, biennials and annuals (which you grow from seed each year), but they often have the greatest impact. They provide colour in every shade and can fill the gaps between other plants or create an ever-changing tapestry of form and texture in a border. Planting a mix of perennials should result in a succession of blooms, as one display is replaced by another.

It is their huge range that makes perennials so invaluable. There are perennials for shade, for full sun, for wet soils or dry soils, and you can find a perennial for every season. They may be low-growing, covering the ground with their foliage, or they may tower above other plants, reaching well over 2m/7ft tall. In a small garden, perennials can be grown in containers, raised beds or along the foot of a wall or fence. In larger spaces, you can create wide borders, line a path with their flowers or plant them around trees or shrubs to create a centrepiece in your garden. There is a perennial for almost every situation.

The variety of perennials also makes it hard to decide what perennials to plant. Think about flowering time, the conditions each plant needs to do well, its height and spread, foliage and flower type. Some perennials are short-lived, flowering for three or four years before giving up, while others can flower for twenty years or more. Above all, think about mixing perennials together, to lengthen the flowering season or create attractive plant associations; introduce a variety of height, foliage or form and enjoy the beauty they bring to a garden.

When gardeners refer to perennials, they usually mean herbaceous perennials but some are evergreen and others are more correctly called subshrubs. All three types are included in this book, but the majority described are herbaceous.

Spilling over the path are these perennial borders, which create a long-lasting parade of colour, and they will flower year after year.

Early-flowering herbaceous perennials, like purple-blue *Salvia nemorosa*, bloom alongside alliums to start the summer display.

Herbaceous perennials

Herbaceous perennials are plants that grow soft stems that last for one growing season before dying down, leaving just the roots to survive until the next season. They do not produce any woody growth above ground. Most are adapted to survive a cold winter, with temperatures falling below freezing. In spring, as temperatures rise and days lengthen, they start to grow, putting up leaves and new stems for the summer ahead.

Some flower early, like bleeding heart (*Lamprocapnos spectabilis*), producing flower buds along with the new leaves, while others may wait until the end of summer to bloom: for example,

Michaelmas daisies (*Symphyotrichum*) and Japanese anemones (*Eriocapitella*).

Herbaceous perennials include many cottage-garden favourites, such as columbines (*Aquilegia*), delphiniums, peonies (*Paeonia*) and phlox. However, a garden planted with herbaceous perennials will have little interest in winter, so fill this seasonal gap with winter and spring bulbs. You can also plant some evergreen perennials to provide some greenery over winter, cover the ground and even contribute a few early flowers.

Evergreen perennials

These perennials hang on to their leaves throughout winter but, like herbaceous perennials, they do not have woody growth above ground. Some may grow their new leaves just as the old leaves are dying back so they are never completely dormant.

Examples of evergreen perennials are Turkish sage (*Phlomis russeliana*), some elephant's ears (*Bergenia*) and coral bells (*Heuchera*). They have leaves year-round and are often grown for their winter foliage, especially the purple-leaved forms of elephant's ears and the patterned cultivars of coral bells.

Some evergreen perennials flower in winter or early spring, including hellebores (*Helleborus*). The leaves of hellebores become leathery as winter approaches, but they are replaced with new leaves, along with the flowers, in late winter. Lungwort (*Pulmonaria*) is semi-evergreen, meaning it loses some leaves but retains a few through winter, and it flowers in early spring.

Subshrubs

Although not always included in a list of perennials, some subshrubs, like penstemons, are grown in the same garden locations and have similar requirements to herbaceous perennials. A subshrub has a small woody framework, but the new growth each year is soft. This growth dies back to the woody stems in winter.

There is no clear distinction between subshrubs and small shrubs. Plants like lavender (*Lavandula*) do have soft new growth, but a greater proportion of these plants develop woody frameworks, especially as they age, and their new growth doesn't die back, so they are better classified as shrubs. Meanwhile, the Mediterranean spurge (*Euphorbia characias*) is an evergreen plant that has a woody base but most of the plant is soft growth so it fits in the subshrub category.

Not everyone will agree, but the subshrubs included in this book are those that fit best, aesthetically and practically, within the range of perennials grown by gardeners.

PERENNIALS IN THE GARDEN

Perennials are highly seasonal, which means they have a distinct appearance for each season of the year. A typical herbaceous perennial might have its main flowering show in summer. In autumn, the stems dry, and the seed heads can look attractive until you cut them back (see Delay cutting back perennials, page 108). In winter, there may be nothing to see, but as spring arrives the bright green new leaves provide a fresh backdrop to spring-flowering bulbs. The value of these seasonal attributes can be used to create an ever-changing display in your garden.

It is tempting to try and plant a year-round border, with something in flower in each season. However, the danger when attempting this is that you end up with year-round mediocrity, with a few flowers at any one time and no peak period. It is better to aim for one peak season so that a border looks amazing for that main display. There can still be flowers to see at other times, but they are not at the expense of the main event.

Aiming for a summer display is probably the easiest option, as the choice of plants is extensive. Fortunately, you can plan a border for other seasons by choosing plants that flower in spring or autumn. There are also several perennials that flower in winter or very early spring, and you can combine these with other plants of winter interest (see Using perennials in a winter garden, page 46). The location of a winter border could be where you can enjoy it from a window so you don't have to go outside to appreciate its beauty. A summer display might be best planted in a part of the garden where you are likely to sit outside on a summer evening.

The amount of light and condition of the soil will influence the choice of plants, as will the style of planting you prefer. This could be a traditional herbaceous border, either in a formal design or the more informal style of a cottage garden, or else be a dry garden, where the soil is free draining and the plants can survive with little watering. Near or under trees, you need plants that tolerate full or partial shade, and in a bog garden the soil is permanently wet, so you should choose plants that thrive in such conditions. Luckily, there are suitable perennials for all these situations.

Herbaceous border

A traditional herbaceous border is the horticultural home of herbaceous perennials. It is often located against a wall or hedge, which provides the backdrop to the planting. In such a position, you can take advantage of the varying heights and foliage types of perennials to create an undulating pattern of leaves and flowers that usually peaks in the summer months. Tall plants near the back of the border can rise to the height of the adjacent hedge or wall (see Planting tall perennials to add height, page 128), while shorter plants produce their flowers nearer ground level.

Small groups of dark blue sage (*Salvia*) and pale pink penstemon, repeated through this border, create a natural, informal design.

A traditional herbaceous border planted against a wall here makes use of the varying heights of perennials to fill the space.

The plants in a border can be arranged in blocks or swathes to make sweeping patterns, or they can be planted in smaller repeating groups (see Repeating plants to unify a border, page 60). Flowers can be grouped together by colour, choosing complementary shades for a more calming effect or opting for contrasting colours to add excitement and drama (see Using colour in a border, page 74). A 'hot' border will have reds, oranges and golden yellows, while a 'cool' border will have more shades of blue, violet, white and pink. A long herbaceous border can change in character along its length, from shocking and vibrant at one end, to calm and soothing at the other. The variety of perennials, especially those that flower in summer, makes almost anything possible when it comes to creating a mood.

Herbaceous borders can also be cut out of a lawn. Because they are surrounded by grass, these are often called island beds; they can be viewed from all sides. Planting tall plants in the centre of an island bed will form a mound, while bringing some taller plants towards the edge creates a more interesting effect. As the bed can be seen from all sides, there is less risk of small plants being hidden by taller forms. Island beds reduce the amount of grass to cut in your garden, and the remaining lawn forms convenient paths that wind around each bed to allow viewing from different angles.

The next logical step is to remove the whole lawn, fill your garden with perennials and lay paths between them made of pavers or stone chips. The paths can be angular and straight, or more curved and sinuous so your perennial planting becomes less formal, as in a gravel garden, meadow or prairie-style design.

Dry garden
In a garden of this type, irrigation is kept to a minimum. The plants are drought tolerant and able to survive without water for several weeks or months. Yet in a climate where rainfall is unpredictable and can occur at any time of year, the plants need protection from excess wet. By incorporating gravel into the soil to improve drainage and by spreading a layer of gravel, at least 5cm/2in thick, over the surface, the plants are kept away from wet ground.

The only watering needed is to help new plants become established, before they have grown their roots down into the soil. In extreme drought, some extra water can be given to the plants, but the idea of a dry garden is to leave them to survive without additional help. This can lead to losses, and some plants may not grow as big as they would in a more traditional garden, but the style of planting becomes more natural looking.

With a varied mix of plants, including bulbs and annuals alongside perennials, a dry garden will behave more like an evolving ecosystem that changes over time. Weeds are less likely to take hold, and plants that are adapted to the conditions will thrive, making a much more sustainable planting scheme that not only reduces water use in your garden but

Plants in a dry garden should be drought tolerant, like this upright myrtle spurge (*Euphorbia rigida*).

also gives a very different appearance to a border.

A gravel garden is the most common type of dry garden. It can be flat or gently undulating, with paths winding between low mounds of soil filled with Mediterranean-climate plants. The thick gravel mulch is a feature of these gardens, but as the plants establish and spread they gradually hide the gravel (see Making a gravel garden, page 68). Low-growing perennials, like smaller sages (*Salvia*) and catmints (*Nepeta*), will encroach along the paths, softening the edges. Prolific self-seeders, like Mexican fleabane (*Erigeron karvinskianus*) and blue vervain (*Verbena hastata*) can colonize the spaces

The shade under trees provides cool conditions that suit a range of woodland plants. Foliage is often just as important as flowers.

between other plants while tall spires of red-hot poker (*Kniphofia*) and mullein (*Verbascum*) add height. A rock garden or raised bed can be planted as a dry garden, too. By raising the planting space above ground, the drainage is improved.

As climate change becomes more advanced, long, hot, dry periods will be more frequent, as will storms and heavy rainfall. In order to survive, a garden will have to cope with these changes and more extreme conditions. A dry garden, with its free-draining soil and drought-tolerant species, will likely become the most common style of garden in areas where traditional

herbaceous borders are currently starting to struggle.

Woodland garden

The opposite to a dry garden or border is a shady woodland one. Here, the amount of shade will have an influence on which plants to grow. Under deciduous trees, the shade may be constant in summer, but once the leaves have fallen in autumn the shade disappears. A border planted along a west- or east-facing wall will be shaded for part of the day – either the morning or afternoon. This is usually referred to as partial shade. Plants will receive plenty of light, especially in the longer days of summer, but can be sheltered from the hottest sun. Partial shade can also refer to the dappled shade under a thin leaf canopy. The sun will reach the ground between the leaves, while there is enough shade cast by the foliage to keep plants cool. Partially shaded borders provide some of the best conditions for a wide range of perennials. There is enough sunlight to prevent them becoming etiolated, and sufficient shade to keep them cool on a hot sunny day.

The soil in a shady border is often moisture-retentive and humus-rich, meaning that it contains a high proportion of decaying leaves and stems, which can make it fertile and give it an open structure. Such moisture-retentive but free-draining soil is the best for a wide range of plants that can be found in sunny or partially shaded herbaceous borders, as well as woodland borders.

Deciduous trees take up a lot of moisture in summer, when they are in full leaf, so the soil can become quite dry. In winter and early spring, before the leaves have unfurled, the soil can be moist and also be exposed to higher light levels. Many plants that are adapted to grow in woodland conditions flower in spring, to take advantage of this light and moisture early in the year. Plants like barrenwort (*Epimedium*) and Solomon's seal (*Polygonatum*) start growing in late winter and flower before the tree leaves shade the ground. In summer, it is often the foliage of shade perennials that makes the best show (see Planting perennials for foliage, page 38). Hostas and rodgersias, for example, have wonderful leaves that can be used to great effect in creating a lush and verdant display.

Bog garden
There may be a part of your garden where the soil never dries out. This is usually

Pink astilbes and yellow leopard plant (*Ligularia*) thrive in the damp soil of a bog garden.

beside a pond or stream but can also be along a ditch or in a shallow depression in the ground, where water gathers and drains away slowly. This permanently damp soil is suitable for growing a number of plants that have adapted to live in marshes or bogs. They are not plants that grow in the water itself, but they do need moist soil year-round. If you have, or can create, the appropriate conditions, you can use moisture-loving plants to make a bog garden.

Plants for a bog garden include the scarlet cardinal flower (*Lobelia cardinalis*), purple loosestrife (*Lythrum*) and yellow loosestrife (*Lysimachia*), meadowsweet

(*Filipendula*) and leopard plant (*Ligularia*). Some irises are adapted to bog garden conditions, like the Japanese water iris (*Iris ensata*) and the yellow flag iris (*I. pseudacorus*).

The location of a bog garden should be where it looks as natural as possible, such as at the foot of a slope or in a natural hollow. Many bog plants need partial shade to prevent their leaves scorching in the midday sun, but if the soil remains damp some plants like purple and yellow loosestrife, cardinal flower and globeflower (*Trollius*) can grow in full sun.

Creating a bog garden can be as simple as clearing and weeding an area that already has permanently wet ground, digging some garden compost into the top 30cm/12in of soil (to increase nutrient levels) and then planting. You can also make a bog garden by using a pond liner to hold water in the soil. Dig a depression in the ground, 30–45cm/12–18in deep, and lay the pond liner over it. Cut a few slits in the liner to allow some water to drain away, otherwise stagnant water will collect. However, it should hold enough water back to keep moisture-loving plants happy. Fill the depression with a mixture of your garden soil and garden compost, and plant into it.

NATURALISTIC PLANTING

In contrast to the formality of a traditional herbaceous border, with its bold groups and carefully curated plant choices arranged according to height, colour and structure, naturalistic planting has a more relaxed approach and aims to look like a plant community. Plants are repeated throughout, either as individuals or in small groups, and mingled together as if they had seeded around randomly. There

is a succession of flowers throughout summer, as different species reach their peak.

Grasses are often an important element of naturalistic planting. They form a backdrop to other plants and bring a different texture and form to a border (see Mixing perennials with grasses, page 118). Small grasses, like prairie dropseed (*Sporobolus heterolepis*), will fill in gaps and still allow plants to grow through and flower without swamping them. This type of planting scheme often mimics a flower meadow or prairie, and it relies on poor soil to inhibit grass growth. When the grasses are cut back, it is important to remove all arisings, as leaving them to decay will add extra nutrients to the soil.

Once the ground for your naturalistic planting scheme has been cleared and the soil lightly turned, leave it until existing weed seeds have germinated so that you can remove them before planting. Further weeding will be necessary until your plants have established.

Choose plants that grow well together and have similar rates of growth so one species doesn't dominate. They all need to be adapted to the same environment, usually full sun and poor soil, and, although annuals and biennials can be included in a naturalistic planting scheme, the majority should be perennials.

This type of planting can be started from seed sown directly on to cleared ground, but you need to be extra vigilant with weeding until your seed has grown into plants that can outcompete the weeds. A more expensive option is to buy plug plants, or you could transplant young plants from elsewhere in your garden, or opt for a combination of seed sowing

Choose a container large enough for your plant when fully grown, like this leafy *Hosta* 'Snowden', which makes an elegant feature in a shady corner.

When grown in pots, less hardy plants like *Salvia* Love and Wishes, can be moved to a sheltered location over winter, for protection.

and introducing plug plants of slower-growing species.

Naturalistic planting doesn't just mean growing native wild flowers. Plants from all over the world can be used if they are suitable. Naturalistic planting is the style of planting – the arrangement of the plants and plant associations. It can mean hundreds of purple coneflowers (*Echinacea*) or black-eyed Susan (*Rudbeckia*) scattered through tufted grass, Joe Pye weed (*Eutrochium*) and patrinias growing with tall grasses, or a mixture of sages (*Salvia*), penstemons and yarrow (*Achillea*) on a sunny slope. Experiment for the best results.

CONTAINERS

Most perennials can be grown in a container, and there are several advantages to this. If the soil in your garden is not suitable for certain perennials, you can grow them in a container, where the soil can be formulated to provide the right conditions. Containers can be moved around so plants in flower are brought out on display and then moved away when they've finished, to be replaced by another one nearing peak interest. In a small garden, containers can be used to decorate a patio, terrace or steps to your door. Plants that are not reliably hardy (see Hardiness zones, opposite) can be put out on display in summer and then moved somewhere more sheltered for winter.

Choosing a suitable container is important. It should be large enough to accommodate the plant when it has reached its mature size. If the container is too small, the soil will dry out quickly and the plant will suffer; if too large, the soil can become waterlogged – especially when the plant isn't taking up enough of the water. Watering and feeding will be necessary, as you need to compensate for the limited nutrient supply and root run the plant will have. A loam-based potting soil is fine for most perennials.

It will hold moisture but allow excess to drain away, as long as your container has holes in the base. For plants that need very free-draining soil, mix one part sharp horticultural sand or sharp grit into two parts loam-based potting soil. This will provide extra drainage for drought-tolerant species that don't like too much moisture in the soil.

Containers can be planted with a single specimen, like a hosta, or you can group a few plants together to make a mini garden (see Planting a container with perennials, page 82). Once they have finished flowering or have past their best,

Hardiness zones

A plant is referred to as hardy if it can survive freezing temperatures. However, some tolerate only a few degrees below freezing while others can live through much colder conditions. In the plant profiles (see pages 30–133), hardiness zones are given for each plant according to the following temperature ranges.

Hardiness zone	Minimum temperature range
H3	+1°C/34°F to −5°C/23°F
H4	−5°C/23°F to −10°C/14°F
H5	−10°C/14°F to −15°C/5°F
H6	−15°C/5°F to −20°C/−4°F
H7	<−20°C/−4°F

The ability of a plant to survive throughout winter is not just about the minimum air temperature. Some may tolerate freezing conditions if the soil is dry or if they are sheltered from the wind. Plants that are reliably covered in snow all winter will freeze but they will not be exposed to extreme cold, as the snow acts like a blanket. Look around your local area to see what plants are surviving in conditions similar to those in your garden.

If you are concerned about a plant's hardiness, place it in a sheltered position, near your house or against a wall that will provide some protection from the wind and may be a few degrees warmer than out in the middle of the garden.

remove the plants from their containers and replant in the garden. The only limit to container gardening is your creativity.

CHOOSING AND BUYING PERENNIALS

Deciding on which perennials to grow can be a daunting task, as the choice is so great. As well as looking through books and magazines for inspiration, visit some gardens at different times of year, make notes and take photographs. Observe gardens in your neighbourhood to see what grows well there and get some ideas. Visit flower shows, where you can see newly introduced varieties as well as old ones grown to perfection. Gradually, you will build up a list of plants you really like and some favourite plant combinations.

If you are starting a new border, try not to buy any plants until you know what you want, however irresistible they might be. At a garden centre you are usually confronted by a wonderful display of in-season flowering plants that suddenly seem to be essential for your border. It is tempting to buy plants before you have worked out your planting plan, but you will end up with whatever was looking good on the day of your garden centre visit, and may discover it doesn't fit with your scheme. This is not such a problem if you are just adding plants to an existing border, because you know what is already growing there, but always make sure any new plants are suitable for the conditions you have.

Also, when buying perennials, don't just get one of each. Think about planting in groups. Depending on their size, you need at least 3–5 of each type to have any impact. A border requires a certain number of plants to fill it, so you are not spending more, just reducing the number of varieties by having more of each one.

If you want to save money, buy plants in small pots. Walk past the seasonal display and head for the herbaceous perennial section in your garden centre. Here, especially in early summer, you can find plants that are not in flower but are large enough to plant out. They might not flower until the following year, but they often establish more quickly and can be less than half the price of bigger specimens. Plants in 9cm/3½in pots, planted in warm autumn soil, will reach the size of a plant in a larger pot by the following summer.

Buying plants out of season is another way to save money. Towards the end of summer, plants are often sold off cheaply. They have finished flowering and may have started to die back, but remember it is the roots you are after. A healthy root system, which you can check by tipping the plant out of its pot, is the most important factor when choosing plants out of season. If the roots are well developed, they should grow successfully when spring comes around.

Splitting plants from a large pot is one way to gain more from a single purchase. This is suitable for clump-forming plants, like phlox or black-eyed Susan (*Rudbeckia*), but not for those that are growing from a single stem. Once home, tip the plant out of its pot and carefully pull it apart to get two or three plants (see Division, page 28).

PLANTING AND AFTERCARE

The best time to plant a perennial is usually autumn. The soil is still warm from the summer, but there is more moisture available. The plants have time

A nursery that propagates and grows its own plants can be an inspiring place to visit and buy plants.

When planting perennials, give them plenty of water to settle the soil around the roots, even if the ground is already damp.

to grow roots into their new soil before winter, and by spring they are ready to grow – and often do so at a surprisingly fast rate. It is a constant source of wonder how a border that looks almost bare in late winter becomes full of leaves and flowers by early summer. Longer days, warmer temperature and spring rains add up to a floral feast as the border erupts into life.

Spring is also a good time to plant. Perennials may take longer to get going but soon catch up. Those in pots can be planted at any time except in winter, when the ground is often too cold and wet, and in summer, when it is too dry. Avoid planting on a hot sunny day or during a period of drought, as this will cause additional stress to the plants. Water new plantings in the early morning or in the evening, to reduce the amount of water lost through evaporation and so allow the plants to get all the moisture they need.

Improving the soil
You may need to amend your soil before planting. Whether you have heavy clay soil or light sandy soil, the best way to improve it is to add organic matter. This can be your own home-made compost or leafmould (see Making your own mulch, page 52). By digging in organic matter, you improve the soil structure, help sandy soils

hold more moisture and enhance drainage in heavy soils. The nutrients present in compost will feed the plants, too.

Planting

Once you have removed any weeds and added organic matter, the soil should be ready for planting. In a new border, position your plants while still in their pots, to make sure they have room to grow and that you are not leaving any large bare patches. The spacings given in the plant portraits (see pages 30–133) are expressed as a range. The higher end of the range gives a more instant display, but after a few years you will probably have to thin out the plants to give the remaining ones more room. The lower end of the scale is the spacing that will result in the plants filling their surroundings in about three years. This is not an exact science and a lot depends on the conditions, the light levels, moisture availability, nutrients, etc., but it is a good guide as to the space each plant will eventually occupy.

When you are happy with the design and spacing of the plants in your border you can start planting. Remove the plants one at a time from their pots and dig a hole for each one in the soil with a trowel. The hole should be about the same depth as the pot. Break up the soil at the base of the hole and place the plant in it. Firm the soil around the plant with your hands, making sure the plant is at the same level in the soil as it was in the pot. Don't bury the base of the plant or leave it sitting above the soil level.

After planting, water the soil around each plant using a watering can or a hose, even if the soil is damp already. The water will cause the soil to settle around the

Mulching a border with garden compost or leafmould helps retain moisture in the soil, reduces weeding and can feed the plants.

roots and remove any air pockets, so apply plenty of it. If you are using a hose, make sure the water pressure is low, so it trickles out gently instead of splashing the soil around. The aim is to make a small puddle of water that will seep into the soil around each plant. If you are planting a lot of new plants in one area, you can wait until you have finished before watering them, but make sure you give each one enough.

Mulching

Once planting is completed, it is a good idea to mulch the surrounding soil. The mulch could be more of your garden compost (see Making your own mulch,

You can buy attractive metal plant supports, like these peony frames, to place over perennials as they start to grow.

deep. Such a deep mulch will prevent weed seeds in the soil from germinating, it will help conserve moisture in the soil, it can add nutrients and, above all, it reduces the need to dig the soil every year. Mulching every winter when your perennials are dormant will make digging unnecessary. Nutrients will seep down from the mulch or be taken down by worms.

If you mulch too early in autumn, the soil may not contain enough moisture after a dry summer so you lose one of the benefits of applying the mulch. If you mulch too late, you risk damaging new shoots or spring bulbs that will be starting to emerge. There is still a reasonably long window in which to apply mulch, from mid-autumn to late winter, but don't mulch frosty ground as it will take longer to thaw.

Support your plants

Once the border or bed is planted and the soil mulched, you can think about staking or installing plant supports. A new border, in its first year, probably won't need much staking, as the plants are still young. However, it is worth making a note over summer of the plants that might require some support the following year. A densely planted border needs less staking as the plants use each other to hold themselves up.

Staking usually takes the form of a cage or frame over the plant, through which the stems then grow and gain support. By summer, the staking should be mostly hidden by the plant. The frame can be made from thin branches of trees or shrubs like hazel (*Corylus*) or birch (*Betula*). Push the branches into the ground around the plant, bend them over and tie together to make the framework.

page 52), and you could use gravel in a dry garden (see page 14). Adding manure to your mulch will provide more nutrients, but it is important that the manure is well-rotted, preferably two or more years old, before you apply it to your borders. Fresh manure can contain pathogens that are harmful to humans, and possibly weedkillers or other chemicals that will damage your plants if the manure has come from animals grazed on treated grass. You can buy ready-rotted manure; if you get fresh manure, find a space to pile it up and leave it to rot down for several years.

Mulching has several benefits, but to be effective it should be at least 10cm/4in

This needs to be done in early spring as the plant is just starting to grow. You can also buy ready-made frames or plant supports, often made of rusted metal or plastic-coated steel rods, that you place around or over the plant. Unlike natural materials, these will last for many years, but they lack the rustic appeal of real branches. You can make frames from willow (*Salix*) stems, woven together to create an attractive structure for supporting plants. They will last two or three years and then need replacing as they gradually fall apart.

Reactive staking is deployed in summer as you see plants starting to fall over under the weight of their flowers. To stop them collapsing completely, push sticks into the ground around the base of the plant, then bend them over to make hoops that offer some support. Willow is useful for this, as it is flexible, but you can also use other branches or sticks that you tie together to form a makeshift frame. Keep a note of the plant needing support so next year you can make its frame before it starts to grow.

In naturalistic planting (see page 17), staking should be avoided if possible. The natural form of the plants is key to the appearance of such planting schemes, and artificial means to hold them up will look out of place. You can always use bamboo canes to tie in individual stems, as long as they are unobtrusive. Delphiniums are a good example of a plant that benefits from a cane holding up its top-heavy flower stem. The cane should hold the stem below the first flowers to give it some rigidity but not be taller than the plant itself.

PROPAGATING PERENNIALS

It takes a lot of perennials to fill a garden. To save having to buy many new plants,

Collect seeds from your garden plants in a paper bag, then keep them cool and dry until ready to sow.

you can try propagating your own to increase your stock. Growing from seed is the slowest method because it can take a few years for seedlings to reach flowering size, but it is the method that will result in the greatest number of new plants, as many seeds can be harvested from a single parent plant. Taking stem or root cuttings is quicker (see pages 27 and 28, respectively). Plants can be flowering the following year, and the technique, at least for some perennials, is quite simple. Dividing perennials is the easiest and quickest method of plant propagation (see page 28), but is suitable only for those plants that form clumps with several growing points. Division also results in the fewest new plants.

You can sow a few seeds in each compartment of a plug tray, but if more than one germinates always remove the spares, so leaving just one to grow on.

Growing from seed

Growing plants from seed that you have collected in your garden is a fun and rewarding way to get more plants, but be aware that many cultivars are the result of complex breeding. The seeds you collect are unlikely to grow into the same plant you collected the seed from, as the characteristics of different hybrids involved in the breeding process will manifest themselves in the seedlings. Sometimes no seed is produced or the seed is sterile and will never germinate. Don't let this put you off. There are cultivars that are selected forms of true species, and their offspring will be fairly similar to the parent plant. The only thing to look out for are hybrids that have occurred in your garden as a result of growing similar plants together. But you never know what you might get so it is worth a go. If you want to grow a particular cultivar from seed, it is better to buy packets of seed from your local garden centre or online. Specific instructions for growing the seeds will be on the packet.

If you decide to collect seed from the plants in your garden, do this by cutting off the seed heads and putting them upside down in a paper bag. Keep in a dry place. The seed will fall out of their pods and collect at the bottom of the bag. You can then discard the stems, pods and any leaves. Clean the seeds further by pouring them into a folded piece of paper and very gently blowing away any debris. The effectiveness of this method will depend on the size of the seed. Very fine seed can be blown away along with the debris so be very careful. You should end up with a small pile of fairly pure seed.

Most seed from perennials is best sown in late winter. By the time it has germinated and grown into a seedling, the day length is longer and the light levels are higher. If you sow them earlier than this you have to nurture tiny seedlings through the cold dark days of winter.

Some seed, especially from plants in the buttercup family (Ranunculaceae) like hellebores (*Helleborus*) and columbines (*Aquilegia*) must be sown as soon as they are ready, to get the best germination rate. If you leave sowing too late, the seed can become dormant, which can be a difficult and slow condition to break. Hellebore seeds often germinate best if taken from the plant when still green, as soon as the seed pod begins to split open.

Sow the seed into small pots, seed trays or plug trays, filled with a seed sowing soil mix. This soil mix will contain appropriate levels of fertilizer for seedlings. If using plug trays, put two or three seeds in each compartment and, if more than one germinates, take out the spares. The first time the pot is watered, place it in a tray of water and allow moisture to soak up from the base until all the soil mix is damp. Afterwards, spray over lightly with water every few days, or more frequently if the weather is warm. Place the seed pots somewhere sheltered from wind and rain, such as an unheated greenhouse or cold frame. If you need to keep them indoors, place in a cool room and out of direct sunlight if possible. You can cover each seed pot or tray with a transparent lid or

When seedlings have grown their first true leaves, you can transfer them into their own pots and grow them on before planting out.

bag to keep the soil mix moist; always remove the covering as soon as the seeds germinate because the humid atmosphere can encourage fungal diseases.

Germination varies from plant to plant. It can take a few days or a few months, but eventually seedlings should grow. Before they get too big, prick out the seedlings into individual pots. This is a delicate process. Handle the seedlings by their leaves only and ease them out of the soil with a stick or dibber. Have a new pot ready filled with more seed sowing soil mix. Make a hole in the new soil and place the seedling in it, gently firming the soil around it. Water it well. After a few weeks you should have vigorous new plants. When you can see roots growing out of the base of the pot, move that seedling into a larger pot filled with standard potting mix. Place outside so it becomes accustomed to the weather before planting out, especially if it has been kept in a greenhouse or indoors. If freezing conditions are forecast, bring it back inside until temperatures are above freezing again. If growth is quick, you may be able to plant it out in the garden after a few more weeks. Otherwise wait until autumn or the following spring.

Stem cuttings
Making new plants by taking shoots or stems, putting them in a pot of soil until they root and then potting them up to plant back in your garden, is the magic of horticulture. Such cuttings can be classified as softwood (using new 'soft' shoots), semi-ripe (from stems that have begun to harden towards the end of summer) and hardwood (cuttings taken in autumn or early winter, from woody stems – a method generally used for shrubs). The cuttings of perennials are usually softwood ones, using new shoots and taken from late spring to late summer (see Taking stem cuttings to get more plants, page 102). Removing faded flower heads can encourage the growth of new shoots that can be used as cutting material towards the end of the summer.

Easy perennials to propagate from cuttings include penstemons, sages (*Salvia*) and catmint (*Nepeta*). Cuttings will be identical to the parent plant so you know what you are getting. You can get a lot of new plants this way if you

The secret to taking successful cuttings is to choose good plant material. Healthy, strong, non-flowering shoots are best, like those on this penstemon.

have plenty of plant material to take the cuttings from.

Plants that form clumps or tufts of mostly basal leaves can be propagated by basal shoot cuttings. Detach a new shoot from the base of the plant and treat it like any other stem cutting. Plants to propagate in this way include delphiniums, lupins (*Lupinus*) and bergamot (*Monarda*).

The most important part of propagating from stem cuttings is to choose strong healthy shoots. Some plants are easier to root this way than others, but if you can find good material you are halfway there. Cut shoots from your plant, preferably on a cool day. Place them in a bag to protect them from drying out too quickly and don't keep them for too long. The quicker you pot them the more likely they will survive. Remove most of the leaves from your cuttings, to reduce the amount of water they lose. Then cut the stem just below a leaf node. This is the point on the stem where the leaves are attached, and this is where cell division is actively occurring and where the roots will develop. Insert the cuttings into seed sowing or cutting soil mix in a pot and water well so all the soil is moist. Place the pot of cuttings out of direct sunlight, in a cold frame, cool greenhouse or windowsill. A cover can help reduce water loss by maintaining a more humid atmosphere, but good material, taken at the right time of year, will root quickly.

Once the cuttings are showing signs of growth, either with new leaves appearing or, more likely, roots growing out of the bottom of the pot, you can pot them individually. If they are strong, you can plant them out in autumn; otherwise wait until spring.

Root cuttings

Not all plants produce suitable shoots for stem cuttings, but you can increase some perennials by root cuttings. These are best taken from late summer to early winter. Perennials that can be propagated from root cuttings include oriental poppies (*Papaver orientale*), some primulas like drumstick primula (*Primula denticulata*), phlox, Japanese anemones (*Eriocapitella*) and mulleins (*Verbascum*).

Dig around the plant to expose some roots. Thicker roots are best. Remove a couple of long roots and cut into 2.5cm/1in lengths, making a right-angled cut where the root was severed from its parent. Then make a sloping cut at the other end of each cutting. Insert the sloping cut end vertically into a pot of seed or cutting soil mix, with the flat end of the root cutting just at soil level. New shoots will grow from this end. By the following spring, the root cuttings should have grown a shoot and you will see new roots emerging from the base of the pot. Transfer the plants individually to new pots, as you would with stem cuttings (see above), and grow them on.

Division

This is a good way to increase plant numbers, spread your favourites around your garden or reinvigorate old specimens. And remember, you can give away divided plants to your friends and neighbours, to spread the joy of your garden further.

Division is suitable for clump-forming plants with several growing points. These include phlox, peonies (*Paeonia*), perennial sunflowers (*Helianthus*), hostas and day lilies (*Hemerocallis*). The process involves digging up the plant and splitting

Root cuttings can be taken from plants that are not easy to propagate from stem cuttings. One long root can make several cuttings.

it, often with a garden fork or spade, into smaller pieces, each with roots and at least one growing point (see Dividing perennials, page 92). The divisions are replanted to spread the plant around or introduce it to another part of your garden. Division is best carried out when the plants are dormant, from autumn to late winter. This will cause the least stress to the plant, and it will be ready to grow once spring comes round again.

Plants like bearded irises and elephant's ears (*Bergenia*) have thick rhizomes near ground level. You can cut off sections of the rhizome to grow on and replant.

Perennials with thick fleshy roots, including peonies and day lilies, need

a little more care to avoid damaging them. The roots can be entwined so you should wash all the soil away and carefully pull the growing points apart, with the fleshy roots attached. Replant them straight away.

Some perennials, like phlox and perennial sunflowers, form expanding clumps that can begin to die out in the middle over time. These benefit from division every few years, to remove the dead centre and reinvigorate the plant by splitting it into smaller pieces, planted in fresh soil.

Division is not suitable for plants that grow from a single point, like mullein (*Verbascum*) or sea kale (*Crambe*), or subshrubs like penstemons.

Plants

Bear's breeches

Acanthus aka bear's breech, bear's britches

These impressive structural plants produce large lobed leaves that cover a wide area. They are sometimes glossy, as in the popular *A. mollis*, and are often spiny. In summer, tall spikes of white flowers with dusky purple bracts reach over a 1m/3ft tall.

—

WHERE TO GROW
Bear's breeches are vigorous plants for tough situations. They do well in full sun and free-draining soil – but will grow in partial shade, especially in warmer climates with long hot summers, such as the Mediterranean region.

HOW TO GROW
Give these plants plenty of room, as the leaves can spread over 1m/3ft across. Once established, bear's breeches need little attention apart from cutting back the leaves if they get too dominant in a border. Some, like *A. spinosus*, are more compact. Propagate by division (see page 28) or root cuttings (see page 28), in late autumn or winter.

GROWING TIP
Bear's breeches have long thick roots so moving them can be difficult, as any roots left behind will grow into new plants.

Family Acanthaceae

Height 1–1.5m/3–5ft

Spacing 1–2 per m²/ 10 sq. ft

Flowering time Summer–autumn

Hardiness Zone 6

ARCHITECTURAL HERITAGE
Acanthus leaves are represented as an ornamental motif on the capitals of Corinthian columns.

Acanthus spinosus

Acanthus mollis

Yarrow

Achillea aka devil's nettle, milfoil, nosebleed plant, soldier's woundwort

Flat or slightly domed heads of many small flowers adorn this colourful group of perennials. They are often low growing but some, like *A. filipendulina*, are tall plants reaching over 1m/3ft. Most have soft, finely divided, grey or green leaves.

—

WHERE TO GROW

Grow the cultivars of yarrow in a sunny position, in moist but well-drained soil. The common yarrow (*A. millefolium*) is a wild flower that can be grown in a meadow. See also Repeating plants to unify a border, page 60.

HOW TO GROW

Yarrow cultivars can survive dry periods but are not especially drought tolerant. Some can be quite short-lived, lasting three to four years, but others, like *A.* 'Moonshine' and *A. filipendulina* 'Gold Plate', are more robust and live longer. Cutting back flowering stems can encourage more vigorous basal growth.

GROWING TIP

Yarrows are best divided in spring (see Dividing perennials, page 92), because if done in autumn the new divisions will not respond well to sitting in cold damp soil over winter, and this may lead to their early demise.

Family	Asteraceae
Height	30–150cm/ 12–60in
Spacing	5–7 per m²/ 10 sq. ft
Flowering time	Summer
Hardiness	Zone 7

NOSEBLEED PLANT
Names like nosebleed plant and soldier's woundwort come from the historical use of yarrow for stopping bleeding.

Achillea millefolium

Achillea 'Paprika'

Monkshood

Aconitum aka common aconite, wolf's bane

Monkshoods produce racemes of hooded flowers above attractive palmate leaves. Commonly deep blue, the flowers can also be pale blue, pink or white, and some, like *A. lycoctonum*, have yellow blooms. All parts are poisonous if digested.

—

WHERE TO GROW

These perennials bring height to a planting but are best shaded from the hottest sun. They often do best in moist soil and partial shade, in an east- or west-facing border.

HOW TO GROW

By planting different species in a mixed herbaceous border, you can spread the flowering season from late spring to late summer. *Aconitum napellus* flowers early while *A. carmichaelii* blooms in late summer. Propagate by division in autumn (see Dividing perennials, page 92); new plants can take a year or two to establish.

GROWING TIP

Use gloves when handling monkshood plants as the poison can be absorbed through broken skin, although incidents are rare.

Family Ranunculaceae

Height 1–1.5m/3–5ft

Spacing 3–5 per m²/ 10 sq. ft

Flowering time Late spring–late summer

Hardiness Zone 7

Aconitum napellus

Aconitum napellus

REGAL STATUS
Aconitine is the most dangerous toxin found in monkshoods and is known as 'the Queen of poisons'.

Baneberry

Actaea aka *Cimicifuga*, bugbane, doll's eye

Baneberries have elegant narrow racemes of small, fragrant, white or pale pink flowers, followed in autumn by clusters of black, red or white, poisonous berries. Some, like *A.* 'Brunette', have dramatic, dark purplish stems and leaves.

—

WHERE TO GROW

Grow in moist fertile soil in the dappled shade of a woodland garden or partially shaded border.

HOW TO GROW

If necessary, improve your soil by digging in or mulching with organic matter, to provide the fertile ground in which baneberries thrive. Give additional watering during dry spells, and shade from hot sun to prevent scorching of the leaves. Divide in early spring (see Dividing perennials, page 92) or grow from seed sown in late winter (see Growing from seed, page 25).

GROWING TIP

The toxic berries look very attractive so don't cut back plants too soon as they extend the season of interest into early winter.

Family Ranunculaceae	
Height 75–150cm/ 30–60in	
Spacing 6–6 per m²/ 10 sq. ft	
Flowering time Summer	
Hardiness Zone 7	

WATCHING YOU
The white fruits on white baneberry (*A. pachypoda*), each with a black spot, have given this plant the name doll's eyes.

Actaea racemosa

Actaea pachypoda berries

Giant hyssop

Agastache aka anise hyssop

Giant hyssop flowers are produced in dense spikes above aromatic foliage. They are commonly blue, but some cultivars, such as the *A.* Kudos Series and *A.* Nectar Series, have flower colours ranging from pink to deep orange-red.

—

WHERE TO GROW

These are plants for a sheltered position in full sun and well-drained soil and can be grown in a border or dry garden.

HOW TO GROW

Taller cultivars, like *A.* 'Blackadder' and *A.* 'Blue Fortune', are hardy, but some of the shorter forms are less so, although they will survive a few degrees of frost. Propagate from softwood cuttings in summer (see Taking stem cuttings to get more plants, page 102). Giant hyssop is sometimes grown as an annual, flowering reliably in its first year.

GROWING TIP

The taller forms, with densely packed flower spikes, can still provide interest once the flowers have faded. Their seed heads combine well with grasses in autumn.

Family Lamiaceae

Height 50–120cm/20–48in

Spacing 3–5 per m²/10 sq. ft

Flowering time Mid–late summer

Hardiness Zone 5–6

: *Agastache* 'Blue Fortune'

TEA BREAK
The leaves of anise hyssop (*A. foeniculum*) can be used to make tea for a cold remedy.

Agastache mexicana

Lady's mantle

Alchemilla

These low-growing plants have beautifully scalloped, soft apple-green leaves and sprays of tiny, greenish-yellow flowers. *Alchemilla mollis* is the most commonly grown. Dwarf lady's mantle (*A. erythropoda*) and alpine lady's mantle (*A. alpina*) are smaller species.

—

WHERE TO GROW

Plant at the front of a border, in sun or partial shade, where lady's mantle can cover the ground. It can colonize paving – its roots reaching between the stones to the moisture below. See also Planting perennials for foliage, page 38.

HOW TO GROW

Lady's mantle is an easy plant to grow and largely pest free. Cut back untidy leaves hard in late summer; replacement leaves will soon grow with renewed freshness. Allow plants to seed around and fill gaps in a border to help smother weeds or spread over cracks in a patio.

GROWING TIP

Plants will quickly multiply so keep them under control by cutting off the flowers before they self-seed and become too invasive.

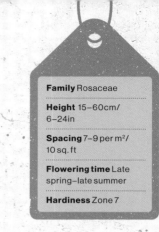

Alchemilla mollis

Alchemilla mollis

FAST TRACK
Many species are apomictic, meaning they can produce seed without the need for fertilization.

Family	Rosaceae
Height	15–60cm/ 6–24in
Spacing	7–9 per m²/ 10 sq. ft
Flowering time	Late spring–late summer
Hardiness	Zone 7

Planting perennials for foliage

When planning what to plant in a border, your primary concern will be the flowers but you shouldn't forget the contribution foliage can make. The leaves of perennials will be around for a lot longer than the flowers, and if you vary the shape and texture of the foliage it can create a pleasing effect before and after the plants have flowered.

Perennials have a wide variety of leaf types, from the long, sword-shaped leaves of irises to the broad ribbed ones of hostas. Low-growing plants, like lady's mantle (*Alchemilla*), barrenwort (*Epimedium*), Turkish sage (*Phlomis russeliana*), lungwort (*Pulmonaria*) and coral bells (*Heuchera*), form useful ground cover that helps prevent weed seeds germinating and fills gaps in a border between other plants. Coral bells have leaves in a range of colours, from bright golden yellow to maroon and deep purple.

Silver or grey foliage often indicates that a plant is drought tolerant, as the leaves are adapted to reflect intense sunlight. Such plants are likely to do well in a dry garden, but plants like the Mediterranean spurge (*Euphorbia characias*) can be grown in any sunny border and its leaves bring another colour to a planting scheme. Mediterranean spurge is evergreen, but herbaceous spurges can also have attractive leaves, like *E. wallichii*, which has narrow green leaves each with a pale central stripe. Some herbaceous perennials, including peonies (*Paeonia*) and blue star (*Amsonia*), have warm autumn colours as they die down.

So, think about foliage when planning a new border or adding new plants to an existing one. Try to vary the types of leaves by introducing different forms and colours. You can create the effect of a verdant jungle or diverse meadow with foliage alone.

A Although there are still some flowers left in this border, it is the variety of foliage that makes the scene, from the wide leaves of Turkish sage to the silvery spurge and fountain of Siberian iris (*Iris sibirica*).

B In a shady border, the wide leaves of *Hosta sieboldiana* bring a green lushness, if you can keep the slugs away.

C The elegant new leaves of barrenwort emerge in late winter. Cut back any old leaves to make way for this fresh young foliage.

D A coral bell and the large leaves of elephant's ear (*Bergenia*) form a dense, weed-suppressing ground cover.

E Blue star (*Amsonia tabernaemontana*) has yellow autumn foliage, here contrasting with the silvery Mediterranean spurge.

Blue star

Amsonia

As their common name suggests, these clump-forming perennials produce panicles of steely blue or white, star-like flowers in early summer. The stems are clothed with narrow leaves that turn golden yellow in autumn.

—

WHERE TO GROW

Blue stars are well suited to an herbaceous border in sun or partial shade. They need moist but well-drained soil and can survive a short period of drought once established. The flowers combine well with other early summer-flowering plants, and the foliage adds texture to a border (see Planting perennials for foliage, page 38).

HOW TO GROW

Once established, blue stars form neat clumps of medium-height stems and need little attention other than cutting back in winter. Propagate by division in early spring (see Dividing perennials, page 92).

GROWING TIP

Grow blue stars alongside later-flowering bulbs, like the taller alliums, to provide an early summer highlight in your garden.

Family Apocynaceae

Height 60–100cm/ 24–39in

Spacing 3–5 per m²/ 10 sq. ft

Flowering time Early–midsummer

Hardiness Zone 5–6

FIT FOR A MAYOR
Amsonia is named after English physician John Amson, who became mayor of Williamsburg, Virginia, in 1750.

Amsonia tabernaemontana

Amsonia tabernaemontana

Columbine

Aquilegia aka granny's bonnet

This easy, well-known garden plant comes in many colours. The distinctive flowers, held on tall wiry stems, have backward-pointing spurs and can be bicoloured. The divided, long-stalked leaves form a loose tuft.

—

WHERE TO GROW

Grow in full sun or partial shade, near the front of a border or scattered through it. Columbine is tolerant of most soil types, except any wet, poorly drained ground.

HOW TO GROW

It is well-known for seeding freely, and plants will turn up unexpectedly around a garden. If you want a particular colour form, grow columbine from bought seed (see Growing from seed, page 25) and plant out in spring or autumn. Some plants have double flowers, like the old cultivar *A. vulgaris* 'Nora Barlow'.

GROWING TIP

To avoid cross-pollination between different forms, divide plants every few years in spring (see Dividing perennials, page 92). Plants will take a while to recover, so look after them.

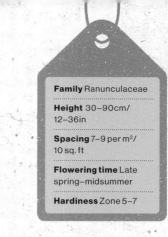

Family Ranunculaceae	
Height 30–90cm/ 12–36in	
Spacing 7–9 per m²/ 10 sq. ft	
Flowering time Late spring–midsummer	
Hardiness Zone 5–7	

Aquilegia coerulea var. *coerulea*

Aquilegia 'Louisiana'

WELL-EARNED REWARD
Columbine spurs contain nectar to attract insects and hummingbirds, which collect pollen as they reach into the base of each flower.

Aster

Aster

The genus *Aster* contains many attractive garden plants but no longer Michaelmas daisies, which are now in a different genus (*Symphyotrichum*). Usually blue, purple or pink, daisy-like flowers appear from midsummer and last well into autumn.

—

WHERE TO GROW

Asters are perfect for an herbaceous border in full sun or partial shade. They do best in fertile, moisture-retentive soil that's not too wet in winter or too dry in summer.

HOW TO GROW

Some asters, like the popular hybrid *A. × frikartii* 'Mönch', can flower for many weeks and fill a gap in the border as earlier flowers fade. Shorter forms are best near the front, but taller cultivars will gracefully reach upwards, supported by surrounded plants.

GROWING TIP

Propagate by division (see Dividing perennials, page 92). After cutting back the old stems, wait until spring to carefully lift and split the clumps, replanting each immediately.

Family Asteraceae

Height 30–90cm/ 12–36in

Spacing 3–5 per m²/ 10 sq. ft

Flowering time Midsummer–autumn

Hardiness Zone 7

COMPOSITE BLOOMS
Aster 'flowers' are actually composed of hundreds of tiny florets: disc florets are in the centre and ray florets around the outside.

Aster amellus

Aster amellus 'King George'

Astilbe

Astilbe aka false goat's beard

Feathery plumes in shades of white, pink, purple and red are held above attractive divided leaves. The more brilliant flowers are too garish for some gardeners, but others appreciate their vibrant colours.

—

WHERE TO GROW

Astilbes need fertile moist soil, near a pond or stream, or other damp, lightly shaded locations. They also grow in a sunny spot if the soil remains damp throughout summer. Shorter forms make good container plants if regularly watered.

HOW TO GROW

In poor soils, add organic matter before planting, to increase fertility and moisture retention. Astilbes are sturdy and do not need staking. Shorter forms make good container plants if regularly watered. Divide every 5–7 years in early spring, to encourage more flowers (see Dividing perennials, page 92).

GROWING TIP

Leave the plumes once flowering is over as the seed heads provide autumn and winter interest in a border.

Family	Saxifragaceae
Height	30–150cm/ 12–60in
Spacing	2–5 per m²/ 10 sq. ft
Flowering time	Midsummer–autumn
Hardiness	Zone 7

Mixed *Astilbe* cultivars

BY GEORG
In the early twentieth century, German nurseryman Georg Arends bred many colourful hybrids called *A. × arendsii*.

Astilbe chinensis

Masterwort

Astrantia aka Hattie's pincushion

Branched stems hold numerous flower heads, each one a ring of prominent bracts around a delicate 'pincushion' of tiny flowers. These blooms are often in shades of white, pink or creamy green, but cultivars like *A*. 'Hadspen Blood' and *A. major* 'Rubra' are deep purple-red.

—

WHERE TO GROW
Plant in a sunny or partially shaded border in humus-rich, moisture-retentive soil. Masterwort can also be grown in a woodland garden in partial but not deep shade.

HOW TO GROW
Masterwort can flower for a few weeks, often with a second flush of bloom in late summer. Cut back after the main flowering period to induce a flush of fresh leaves and flowers. Propagate by division in early spring (see Dividing perennials, page 92) or by seed sown in late summer (see Growing from seed, page 25).

GROWING TIP
These plants seed themselves around and, once established, can be difficult to remove as their roots are tough. Therefore, selectively thin out seedlings in a border.

Astrantia 'Buckland'

Family Apiaceae

Height 30–90cm/ 12–36in

Spacing 5–7 per m²/ 10 sq. ft

Flowering time Mid–late summer

Hardiness Zone 7

OLD FAVOURITE
Masterwort has been grown in gardens since at least the sixteenth century.

Astrantia maxima

False indigo

Baptisia aka false lupine, wild indigo

Tall spires of well-spaced, usually blue, pea-like flowers are borne above leaves each comprising three leaflets. Because false indigo is increasingly popular, new cultivars have been developed in flower colours varying from purple to pink, white and yellow.

—

WHERE TO GROW

Plant in full sun and well-drained soil in a sunny herbaceous border. False indigo is drought resistant once established.

HOW TO GROW

Space plants at least 60cm/2ft apart because growth continues after flowering, making significant clumps. The attractive foliage and inflated seed pods add interest to a border right though to autumn. Strong plants can be divided in autumn or winter (see Dividing perennials, page 92), but generally false indigo doesn't like disturbance, so propagation by seed is preferable (see Growing from seed, page 25).

GROWING TIP

The leaves will blacken after frost so cut them back to ground level in autumn. New shoots will quickly grow in spring.

Baptisia sphaerocarpa
'Screamin' Yellow'

Family	Fabaceae
Height	1–1.25m/3–4ft
Spacing	2–3 per m²/ 10 sq. ft
Flowering time	Early summer
Hardiness	Zone 7

TO DYE FOR
Baptisia australis is called blue false indigo because a blue dye can be made from its roots.

Baptisia australis

45

Using perennials in a winter garden

Most perennials flower from late spring to early autumn and then die down, but there are a select few that flower in the depths of winter or have attractive berries. These can bring some colour to a garden in the coldest months of the year. The common primrose (*Primula vulgaris*) appears early and can be grown in a border or a lawn, displaying its soft yellow blooms. It will seed around, too, and mix well with lungwort (*Pulmonaria*), another early perennial. The evergreen stinking iris (*Iris foetidissima*) has bright orange berries and the Algerian iris (*I. unguicularis*) has violet-blue winter flowers.

Some of the most beautiful, winter-flowering perennials are hellebores, with their saucer-shaped flowers in pastel shades. The Christmas rose (*Helleborus niger*) is named for its mid-winter flowering. From mid- to late winter, hellebores push their flowers upwards from between the stalks of the old foliage. It is a good idea to cut back these old leaves to show off the new blooms. Be careful when cutting not to damage the soft new shoots. It is advisable to wear gloves to avoid accidentally cutting your fingers.

Evergreen foliage is invaluable for softening a winter garden. Some large-leaved plants, like elephant's ears (*Bergenia*), can also bring colour. *Bergenia purpurascens* has purple foliage, and in winter the colour is deeper. The leaves glow in the light of the low sun. The silvery leaved Mediterranean spurge (*Euphorbia characias*) has beautiful leafy stems, and from the middle of winter the tips begin to arch over as the flowers develop. This wonderful plant brings both colour and texture to a border even before the flowers open.

Plant these winter perennials to complement the coloured stems of dogwoods (*Cornus*) and willows (*Salix*). Add some winter bulbs, like snowdrops (*Galanthus*) and winter aconites (*Eranthis*), and you will have a border to enjoy as you wait for spring.

A Hellebores are some of the most beautiful of winter-flowering perennials. After flowering is over, carefully cut away the old leaves as the new shoots grow. Removing the old leaves of hellebores will show off the flowers nicely and removes any diseased foliage. New leaves grow along with the flowers.

B The common primrose flowers in late winter. It can be left to seed around, often appearing in a lawn or under shrubs.

C This planting of purple-leaved elephant's ears with a warm glow complements the red stems of dogwoods in the Winter Garden at Wakehurst Place in West Sussex, UK.

D The leafy stems of the Mediterranean spurge arch over as the flowers buds develop.

Elephant's ears

Bergenia aka large rockfoil

These tough, evergreen, ground-cover perennials
have thick rhizomes and large, rounded, leathery
leaves. Some, like *B. purpurascens*, develop attractive
winter foliage. Clusters of white or pink flowers open
on upright stems from early spring.

—

WHERE TO GROW

Grow elephant's ears in a variety of locations in
sun or partial shade at the front of a border or on
a slope. It makes good ground cover in poor soils
or under trees.

HOW TO GROW

Use these reliable plants to fill gaps between taller
perennials or shrubs, as they tolerate shade and are
drought resistant once established. They are also
valued for their weed-suppressing foliage,
while those with purple leaves are often chosen
for winter gardens (see Using perennials in a
winter garden, page 46). Propagate by cutting
off rooted sections of rhizome in late spring
or autumn and replanting (see Dividing
perennials, page 92).

GROWING TIP

Cut off damaged leaves in late summer
or in early spring, to make way for fresh new
leaves to accompany the flowers.

Family Saxifragaceae

Height 30–60cm/
12–24in

Spacing 5–7 per m²/
10 sq. ft

Flowering time
Early–late spring

Hardiness Zone 6–7

FAMILY RESEMBLANCE

Elephant's ears are in the same
family as rockfoils (*Saxifraga*),
hence its other common name –
large rockfoil.

*Bergenia
purpurascens*

Bistort

Bistorta aka *Persicaria*, knotweed

These vary from bulky herbaceous perennials over
1m/3ft tall to creeping ground-cover plants. They
have thin dense spikes of flowers from summer
through to autumn, in shades of pink, purple, red or
white, held above the leaves.

—

WHERE TO GROW

Plant in moisture-retentive soil in full sun, although
bistort tolerates partial shade. Many are late
flowering, so ideal for an herbaceous border.

HOW TO GROW

The most commonly grown are the many cultivars
of *B. amplexicaulis* (syn. *Persicaria amplexicaulis*),
which are large, clump-forming plants that take up
a lot of space in a border. They are semi-evergreen
but the leaves can look untidy, so cut the stems
back to ground level after flowering. Propagate
by division in autumn (see Dividing perennials,
page 92).

GROWING TIP

Low creeping forms, such as *B. affinis* and
B. vacciniifolia, can be grown over a wall or rocks,
where they will form a mat covered in flower spikes.

Family Polygonaceae

Height 30–150cm/
12–60in

Spacing 3–5 per m²/
10 sq. ft

Flowering time Late
summer–autumn

Hardiness Zone6

SYNONYMOUS
Although their name has
changed, you'll still find many
popular garden forms of bistort
under their previous name,
Persicaria, in some garden
centres and nurseries.

Bistorta affinis

*Bistorta
amplexicaulis*

Siberian bugloss

Brunnera aka Siberian bugloss

The renowned gardener and writer Christopher Lloyd described Siberian bugloss as 'a useful plant for the bored gardener' and they do have value as ground cover for shaded areas. Large , heart-shaped leaves are topped by sprays of blue, forget-me-not flowers in spring. Cultivars like *B. macrophylla* 'Jack Frost' have attractively variegated foliage.

—

WHERE TO GROW

Siberian bugloss is best planted in cool partial shade, but can be grown in full sun if the soil remains damp – but the leaves can scorch. It is a great plant for filling in under trees or around shrubs, flourishing in shade and keeping down weeds. It is also good for a woodland garden or shady border.

HOW TO GROW

This long-lived and slow spreader needs moisture-retentive soil to thrive, so dig in some organic matter if necessary before planting. It is easily increased by division in autumn (see Dividing perennials, page 92).

GROWING TIP

Plant with spring bulbs, like tulips, which will push through the Siberian bugloss leaves and hold their blooms above the sprays of blue flowers.

Family	Boraginaceae
Height	30–45cm/ 12–18in
Spacing	5–7 per m²/ 10 sq. ft
Flowering time	Spring
Hardiness	Zone 6

Brunnera macrophylla 'Jack Frost'

TURKISH DELIGHT
Although called Siberian bugloss, the most common species, *B. macrophylla*, comes from Turkey and the Caucasus.

Brunnera macrophylla

Bellflower

Campanula

This large and varied group of plants includes annuals, biennials and alpines. The best of the perennial bellflowers are tall, graceful, floriferous plants with bell- to star-shaped flowers in summer. The blooms are often in a shade of blue, while pinks, purples and whites are not uncommon.

WHERE TO GROW
Plant the taller perennials, like *C. lactiflora*, in fertile, moisture-retentive soil, in a sunny or partially shaded border; they dislike winter wet. Try shorter forms at the front of a border or in a raised bed.

HOW TO GROW
Removing spent flowers may promote a second flush of blooms. Divide in autumn (see Dividing perennials, page 92) or allow to seed around.

GROWING TIP
Ground-hugging forms, like *C. poscharskyana*, can be grown in paving, dry-stone walls and rock gardens, where they will hang down or spread along cracks.

Family Campanulaceae

Height 20–180cm/ 8–72in

Spacing 5–9 per m²/ 10 sq. ft

Flowering time Summer

Hardiness Zone 7

MEADOW FLOWER
The delicate-looking harebell, *C. rotundifolia*, is a plant of grassland, cliff tops and heaths in cool temperate regions.

Campanula rotundifolia

Campanula lactiflora

Making your own mulch

Different materials can be used to mulch a border, but organic material, like well-rotted manure, leafmould and composted garden waste, are great for a woodland garden or herbaceous border (see also Mulching, page 22). Although you can buy mulch in bags, it is far more satisfying to make your own. Recycling plant material to use as a soil mulch helps to keep carbon in the garden, returning it to the soil and feeding your plants, while preserving the soil's ecosystem.

If you pile plant material in the corner of your garden, it will slowly rot down. After several months, you can extract compost from the base of the pile. This isn't the tidiest or quickest way to make compost but it does work. To speed things up, use a container of some sort that keeps the compost heap neat and allows you to get in with a garden fork to turn it over every week or so. This will speed up the decomposition process.

Try and mix the material you add to your compost bin. Using just grass clippings, for example, will create a slimy mess. The dried stems and leaves of a variety of plants help to make compost with a crumbly texture. If you have a lot of grass clippings, you can add cardboard to the pile, to absorb some of the moisture and make air pockets in the heap, to help with decomposition.

Leafmould is made from fallen tree leaves. Collect these and put them in a compost bin or make a chicken wire enclosure for them. Alternatively, put damp leaves in a plastic bin liner with a few holes in the sides. After a year or two, you should have a fine-textured leafmould, which is great for adding to potting soil or for applying as a mulch.

A Collect plant material from your garden to fill a container and let it rot down. Turning it regularly with a garden fork will speed up decomposition.

B Garden waste can be piled in a corner, and even if you just leave it alone it will rot down and create useful compost that you can extract from the bottom of the pile.

C A good-quality garden compost is dark coloured and has a moist crumbly texture. Pick out any thick roots or sticks that haven't decomposed.

D In a small border, you can fill a pot with compost and spread it between the plants as a mulch.

E In a large border, it is quicker to use a wheelbarrow to move the mulch to where it is needed. Stand on wooden planks to reduce compaction of the soil.

Giant scabious

Cephalaria aka tree scabious, yellow scabious

Perennial species of giant scabious form tufts of pinnately divided leaves with wiry wafting stems that display creamy yellow, occasionally blue, scabious-like flowers from early summer. *Cephalaria gigantea* can reach 2m/7ft tall, and other species like *C. alpina* and *C. balansae* are only slightly shorter.

—

WHERE TO GROW

Grow in a sunny herbaceous border in moisture-retentive but free-draining soil, sheltered from strong winds.

HOW TO GROW

Giant scabious are mostly tall plants for the back of a border and look very effective with tall grasses (see Planting tall perennials to add height, page 128; and Mixing perennials with grasses, page 118). The stems are self-supporting except in exposed windy sites, where some staking will be needed. They can slowly spread by self-sown seed.

GROWING TIP

Plants grown from seed sown under glass in winter can flower within 6–8 months (see Growing from seed, page 25). Otherwise, sow in spring for flowers the following summer.

Family Caprifoliaceae	
Height 1.5–2m/5–7ft	
Spacing 1–3 per m²/ 10 sq. ft	
Flowering time Summer	
Hardiness Zone 7	

Cephalaria gigantea

ONE IN A HUNDRED

Out of a hundred species in the *Cephalaria* genus, *C. gigantea* is the one you are most likely to come across in gardens.

Cephalaria leucantha

Plume thistle

Cirsium aka brook thistle, melancholy thistle

Cirsium is a large genus of thistle-like plants.
Those grown ornamentally have only moderately
spiky leaves and display attractive thistle heads of
deep purple or reddish-maroon flowers that peer
above surrounding plants on tall, upright, mostly
leafless stems.

WHERE TO GROW

Grow plume thistle in a sunny herbaceous border in
moisture-retentive but well-drained soil. It tolerates
short periods of drought.

HOW TO GROW

Plume thistle looks best when growing among other
perennials, such as penstemons (see page 107),
cranesbill (*Geranium*; see page 72) or the foliage of
later-flowering plants like milk parsley (*Ligusticopsis
wallichiana*). It can seed around so cut off the flowers
once finished, to keep it under control. Propagation
is easiest from seed sown in late winter (see Growing
from seed, page 25).

GROWING TIP

If the stems are cut back after flowering, there
can be a second flush of bloom in late summer.

Family	Asteraceae
Height	75–120cm/ 30–48in
Spacing	2–3 per m²/ 10 sq. ft
Flowering time	Early–midsummer
Hardiness	Zone 7

CHEER UP!
A potion made from
melancholy thistle
(*C. heterophyllum*) was
believed to cure sadness.

*Cirsium
rivulare*

Cirsium rivulare 'Atropurpureum'

Sea kale

Crambe aka sea cabbage

These are big perennials, with beautifully glaucous, edible, cabbage-like leaves. European sea kale (*C. maritima*) has clusters of white, honey-scented flowers in early summer and greater sea kale (*C. cordifolia*), from the Caucasus and farther east, produces huge panicles of small, creamy white flowers.

Family Brassicaceae	
Height 0.75–1.8m/ 2½–6ft	
Spacing 1–3 per m²/ 10 sq. ft	
Flowering time Spring–early summer	
Hardiness Zone 7	

WHERE TO GROW

Sea kale needs full sun and deep, well-drained soil. Greater sea kale is a big plant for the back of a border, with its panicles of flowers reaching nearly 2m/7ft. European sea kale is shorter but still forms a prominent cluster of large, distinctively blue-grey leaves, and it does well in a dry garden.

HOW TO GROW

Grow from seed that has been soaked overnight and scratched to break the hard outer coat. Sow the seed in late autumn or winter (see Growing from seed, page 25). Once established, plants are hard to move as they have long thick roots.

GROWING TIP

Sea kale can also be propagated from root cuttings in in winter or early spring (see Root cuttings, page 28).

Crambe maritima

Crambe maritima

LIFE'S A BEACH
European sea kale is usually found growing in shifting shingle along the coast, anchored by its deep roots.

Delphinium

Delphinium

This classic border perennial has seen much breeding over the years, resulting in stunning plants with tall candles of densely packed blooms. Flowers are usually rich dark to light blue, with contrasting, dark or white centres, but can also be pink, purple or white.

—

WHERE TO GROW

The perennial delphiniums are best suited to herbaceous borders in full sun, with fertile soil that retains some moisture but is never waterlogged.

HOW TO GROW

Delphiniums need space and are best when not crowded by other plants. The tall flower spikes can fall over under the weight of blooms, especially in windy conditions, so tie each spike to a single stake, just shorter than the spike, to hold it up. Remove the stake and cut back the stems after flowering.

GROWING TIP

Take softwood cuttings in spring, once growth starts, by cutting off new shoots where they join the rootstock (see Stem cuttings, page 27). Sow seed in late winter (see Growing from seed, page 25).

Family Ranunculaceae	
Height 0.75–2m/2½–7ft	
Spacing 3–5 per m²/ 10 sq. ft	
Flowering time Early–midsummer	
Hardiness Zone 5–6	

Delphinium elatum

POD LIFE
Delphinium comes from *Delphis*, meaning dolphin, as the shape of the spurred flower is vaguely similar.

Mixed *Delphinium* cultivars

Foxglove

Digitalis

Although best known for the biennial *D. purpurea*, there are also several perennial species that form a rosette of leaves and upright racemes of tube-shaped flowers in various colours from yellow and pink to rusty brown.

—

WHERE TO GROW

These adaptable plants can be grown in partial shade or full sun, in well-drained but moisture-retentive soil. Those from the Mediterranean region, like *D. ferruginea* and *D. parviflora*, are drought tolerant and do well in a dry garden, often seeding around.

HOW TO GROW

Most species of foxglove are easily raised from seed sown in late winter (see Growing from seed, page 25). Division of larger clumps in early spring is possible but not always successful (see Dividing perennials, page 92).

GROWING TIP

Plants are toxic if ingested so handle with care, and wash your hands thoroughly after handling.

Family Plantaginaceae

Height 30–60cm/ 12–24in

Spacing 5–7 per m²/ 10 sq. ft

Flowering time Spring–midsummer

Hardiness Zone 5–6

Digitalis ferruginea

Digitalis ferruginea

DO OR DIE
Digitalis is a drug used to treat heart conditions under strict medical supervision, but in the wrong dose it can be fatal.

Coneflower

Echinacea aka purple coneflower

Large, daisy-like flowers with prominent central cones are produced on these popular plants from midsummer. The blooms are mostly in shades of purple, deep pink or white, but some recent cultivars have orange, red or yellow flowers. They can continue flowering into autumn.

WHERE TO GROW

They do well in moist, free-draining soil, and are perfect herbaceous border plants, flowering best in full sun. Some, like *E. pallida*, are suitable for prairie-style planting (see Mixing perennials with grasses, page 118). Avoid planting in soil that is waterlogged in winter.

HOW TO GROW

Coneflowers are good mixers in a border, flowering alongside other late summer perennials, like black-eyed Susans (*Rudbeckia*; see page 120) and *Crocosmia* or ornamental grasses. They need plenty of sunshine so make sure they are not crowded out. Avoid planting in soil that is waterlogged in winter. Propagate by division in spring (see Dividing perennials, page 92).

GROWING TIP

Some of the newer cultivars are not long-lived, fading away after a year or two. Check plant awards and trials, like those run by the Royal Horticultural Society, to find the best forms.

Family Asteraceae

Height 60–100cm/ 24–39in

Spacing 3–5 per m²/ 10 sq. ft

Flowering time Midsummer–early autumn

Hardiness Zone 5–6

Echinacea pallida

HEALING POWERS
Echinacea is one of the most popular herbal remedies used to treat the common cold and flu.

Echinacea purpurea

Repeating plants to unify a border

There are design principles you can apply to improve the look of a border. One of the most effective is the repetition of plants to bring unity to a planting scheme. The repeated plants give a more harmonious appearance to a border, bringing all the plants together by having a few that occur more than once. A random jumble of plants suddenly becomes a coherent scheme.

The plants you choose to repeat can be the same colour, have the same foliage or the same flower type. The architectural form of some spurges (*Euphorbia*) can be used or the brightly coloured flowers of a penstemon. These can be placed at regular intervals to lead the eye along a border or be scattered through other plants to tie them all together.

The effect of repetition may be seasonal. For example, black-eyed Susan (*Rudbeckia*) will flower in late summer, and two or three groups of this will have the desired impact. In the same border, a similar effect can be achieved in early summer with blue sages, like *Salvia nemorosa* 'Caradonna' and *S.* × *sylvestris* 'Mainacht'. If the general appearance is the same, the plants don't have to be the same variety. Yarrow (*Achillea*) will work in different colours, because the form and the flower type are similar.

The good news is that you don't have to clear a border and start again. Just buy a few plants of the same variety or form, clear two or more spaces in the existing border and add your new plants. They will make a difference. If you are replanting a border completely, think of two or three different plants you can repeat, to create the effect at different times of the year or to provide a structural element even when the plants are not in flower.

A   In early summer, repeating groups of blue salvias, yellow Turkish sage (*Phlomis russeliana*) and maroon plume thistle (*Cirsium rivulare* 'Atropurpureum') create a coherent design.

B   Regularly spaced structural plants, like the Mediterranean spurge (*Euphorbia characias*), lead the eye through a planting scheme.

C   The plants along this path are varied but repeating features, like the blue flowers of catmint (*Nepeta*) and lavender (*Lavandula*) and the distinctive blooms of globe thistle (*Echinops*) on either side, bring the mix of plants together.

D   Just two prominent groups of the coneflower *Echinacea purpurea* 'White Swan', along with blue *Agapanthus*, are enough to bind this planting scheme together.

E   The swathes of black-eyed Susan (*Rudbeckia fulgida*) on the Great Broad Walk Borders at the Royal Botanic Gardens, Kew, demonstrate repetition on a grand scale.

Globe thistle

Echinops

The perennial globe thistles have metallic blue, spherical or globe-shaped flower heads, each made up of many small tubular blooms. They look like spiny balls until the starry flowers open. Their leaves are thistle-like, spiny and often grey-green.

—

WHERE TO GROW
Plant in a sunny border, in free-draining soil. Globe thistle can also be grown in a dry garden.

HOW TO GROW
Position towards the back of a border, as the leaves can look scruffy by the second half of summer. Shorter perennials should hide the lower foliage, leaving the rounded flower heads bobbing above other plants. Once established, globe thistle is drought tolerant and can self-seed.

GROWING TIP
Propagate established clumps by division in autumn or spring (see Dividing perennials, page 92), or by root cuttings taken in late winter (see Root cuttings, page 28).

Family Asteraceae

Height 60–150cm/ 24–60in

Spacing 3–5 per m²/ 10 sq. ft

Flowering time Flowering time Mid–late summer

Hardiness Zone 7

PRICKLES
Echinops comes from the Greek *echinos*, meaning hedgehog, as the flower heads are like prickly balls.

Echinops bannaticus 'Taplow Blue'

Echinops ritro

Barrenwort

Epimedium aka bishop's hat

Delicate sprays of intriguing, star-like flowers are borne in spring on these low-growing, deciduous or evergreen perennials. New leaves are often attractively patterned or flushed with bronzy red as they emerge in early spring. See also Planting perennials for foliage, page 38.

—

WHERE TO GROW
Barrenwort will cover the ground when growing in moist but well-drained, humus-rich soil in a shady bed or woodland garden, and some, like *E. pinnatum*, survive in dry shade. All will be scorched by hot sun.

HOW TO GROW
Plant barrenwort under a deciduous tree, around a shrub or at the front of a border. This rhizomatous plant forms a spreading clump or mat of foliage that is easy to divide in autumn (see Dividing perennials, page 92).

GROWING TIP
Although evergreen forms retain their leaves through the winter, their foliage is best cut back before fresh new shoots and flower stems start growing in early spring.

Family	Berberidaceae
Height	25–60cm/ 10–24in
Spacing	7–9 per m²/ 10 sq. ft
Flowering time	Spring
Hardiness	Zone 6–7

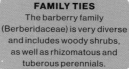

FAMILY TIES
The barberry family (Berberidaceae) is very diverse and includes woody shrubs, as well as rhizomatous and tuberous perennials.

Epimedium × perralchicum

Epimedium pinnatum

Fleabane

Erigeron aka beach aster, Mexican fleabane

These mostly compact plants display daisy-like flowers, often in pink or purple with yellow centres. Several cultivars are available, but the most commonly grown species is Mexican fleabane (*E. karvinskianus*), which produces masses of white flowers on airy stems.

—

WHERE TO GROW

Grow at the front of a border or raised bed, in full sun. Mexican fleabane can colonize steps and walls and thrives in a dry garden.

HOW TO GROW

Plant in well-drained soil, adding some grit to improve drainage if necessary. Soil that retains some moisture in summer will be beneficial for many fleabane, but Mexican fleabane can survive harsh conditions and will seed around, seeking out cracks and crevices, where it will flower all summer.

GROWING TIP

Sow seed in late winter (see Growing from seed, page 25) or take softwood cuttings from mat-forming fleabanes, like *E. glaucus*, in spring (see Taking stem cuttings to get more plants, page 102). Broader clumps can be divided in autumn or spring (see Dividing perennials, page 92).

Family	Asteraceae
Height	15–75cm/ 6–30in
Spacing	7–9 per m²/ 10 sq. ft
Flowering time	Summer
Hardiness	Zone 5

Erigeron speciosus

Erigeron karvinskianus

REPELLENT
Several plants are named fleabane, suggesting they repel fleas, although it probably refers to a particularly smelly tropical species.

Japanese anemone

Eriocapitella aka *Anemone*, Japanese windflower

These tall, late-summer perennials have a succession of wide, saucer-shaped flowers in shades of magenta, pink and white, with a boss of yellow stamens in each centre.

—

WHERE TO GROW

Japanese anemones bring late colour to an herbaceous border or woodland garden, in moist but free-draining soil that doesn't dry out in summer. They can grow in sun or partial shade but suffer in drought, and the leaves can be scorched by hot midday sun.

HOW TO GROW

Flower stems can reach over 1m/3ft tall so plant where you need some height. Japanese anemone can easily spread, and the best way to control it is to lift and split up each clump in spring (see Dividing perennials, page 92).

GROWING TIP

The seeds of these anemones are clustered together in fluffy white balls, like cotton wool. When grown from seed, they can take several years to flower (see Growing from seed, page 25).

| Family Ranunculaceae |
| Height 1–1.5m/3–5ft |
| Spacing 3–5 per m²/ 10 sq. ft |
| Flowering time Late summer–autumn |
| Hardiness Zone 7 |

Eriocapitella japonica

Eriocapitella hupehensis

TURNING JAPANESE
These anemones are not native to Japan but have escaped from gardens there, from where they were sent to Europe.

Sea holly

Eryngium aka eryngo

These spiky, thistle-like plants have been bred to form ever more intensely blue flower heads. It is the bracts that have the most colour, surrounding a small domed umbel of flowers.

—

WHERE TO GROW

Plant in full sun in a well-drained border, coastal or dry garden. Sea holly can also be used with grasses in prairie-style planting (see Mixing perennials with grasses, page 118). Many of the perennial species used in gardens are from climates with hot dry summers.

HOW TO GROW

Sea hollies are adaptable to a range of conditions, as long as they get enough sunshine and the soil is never waterlogged. Some species, like *E. yuccifolium*, can reach over 1m/3ft tall. Ensure smaller forms are not overcrowded by other plants.

GROWING TIP

Deep taproots make some sea hollies hard to move so propagate them by seed sown in late winter (see Growing from seed, page 25) or by root cuttings in early spring (see Root cuttings, page 28).

Family Apiaceae	
Height 45–120cm/ 18–48in	
Spacing 3–5 per m²/ 10 sq. ft	
Flowering time Summer	
Hardiness Zone 5	

Eryngium yuccifolium

SEASIDE ROMANCE
True sea holly (*E. maritimum*) has edible roots and flowers that were once thought to be an aphrodisiac.

Eryngium bourgatii

Spurge

Euphorbia

Among over 2,000 species of *Euphorbia*, the perennial garden spurges are some of the best foliage plants for a border. Leaves may be lush green with a pale central stripe or strikingly glaucous. Tiny flowers are surrounded by acid-yellow, orange or pale green bracts.

—

WHERE TO GROW

There are spurges for sun and shade. Plant shade-tolerant spurges, like *E. griffithii*, in humus-rich, moisture-retentive soil. Sun-loving species, like *E. characias* and *E. rigida*, need well-drained soil and are often drought tolerant. Most spurges are suitable for an herbaceous border, and some Mediterranean species, like *E. myrsinites*, will do well in a dry garden. (See also Using perennials in a winter garden, page 46; and Planting perennials for foliage, page 38.)

HOW TO GROW

Many spurges are evergreen and just need tidying in late summer by removing the finished flower heads. Cut back herbaceous species in late autumn.

GROWING TIP

Divide spreading forms, like *E. cyparissias* and *E. amygdaloides,* in autumn (see Dividing perennials, page 92). Propagate evergreen spurges from stem cuttings in early summer (see Taking stem cuttings to get more plants, page 102) but beware of the milky sap (see below).

Euphorbia griffithii 'Fireglow'

Family Euphorbiaceae
Height 30–150cm/ 12–60in
Spacing 2–5 per m²/ 10 sq. ft
Flowering time Early spring–summer
Hardiness Zone 5–7

BEWARE
The milky white sap produced by spurges can irritate the skin, eyes and mouth, so handle this plant with gloves.

Euphorbia rigida

Making a gravel garden

A gravel garden is a place to grow plants that are used to prolonged periods of drought. Once established, they rely on natural rainfall to provide the moisture they need and so help you reduce water usage in your garden. Where rainfall is unpredictable and can occur at any time of year, the gravel ensures the soil drains quickly and plants are not left sitting in wet ground.

The plants to grow in a gravel garden are typically from places that experience a long dry summer, such as the Mediterranean region. They will be used to high levels of sunlight so the location of a gravel garden should be in full sun. In heavy soil, incorporate sharp horticultural grit into the top 15–30cm/6–12in of soil. It should be angular and 3–6mm/⅛–¼in in diameter.

The most important element of a gravel garden is the mulch of gravel you lay over the soil surface. This layer can be up to 10cm/4in thick and provides a very free-draining layer that will keep your plants free from wet soil. The gravel for the mulch layer can be varied in size, to create a natural-looking surface.

In a new gravel garden, first dig in the plants, setting them a little higher than normal in the soil, then add the gravel mulch, which will cover the roots. Until their roots have grown into the soil, new plants need watering in dry spells.

A Use sharp horticultural grit of 3–6mm/⅛–¼in to improve drainage in the top layer of soil and as mulch for small plants or those with small leaves.

B Larger gravel, or stones of mixed sizes, can be used as mulch to create a more natural appearance around plants. Eventually the plants should cover most of the gravel.

C When planting in an existing gravel garden, first remove the layer of mulch to expose the soil beneath. Plant into the soil and then push the gravel mulch back underneath the leaves.

D There are many perennials that will survive drought. Mix them with bulbs, grasses and small shrubs to create a colourful garden with a Mediterranean feel.

E The upright myrtle spurge (Euphorbia rígida) is a great plant for a gravel garden and a good example of one that needs a thick mulch to keep its fleshy stems away from moisture.

F Giant hyssops, like Agastache 'Blue Fortune', are drought-tolerant plants that flower in late summer.

Joe Pye weed

Eutrochium aka *Eupatorium*

Joe Pye weed is a towering upright perennial with clouds of purplish flowers held in domed heads on leafy stems up to 2.5m/8ft tall.

WHERE TO GROW

Soil should be moisture-retentive and free-draining, although Joe Pye weed can also grow in poor soils. Plant in a border in full sun; in partial shade, Joe Pye weed may lean towards the light.

HOW TO GROW

Position where you need height, at the back of a border or as a screen (see Planting tall perennials to add height, page 128). Joe Pye weed combines well with tall grasses. Divide large clumps in autumn when you cut back the stems (see Dividing perennials, page 92). Joe Pye weed is not classed as invasive, but it can slowly spread by self-sown seedlings.

GROWING TIP

Remove the spent flower heads once the colour has faded, to prevent them seeding around.

Eutrochium maculatum

Family	Asteraceae
Height	1.25–2.5m/4–8ft
Spacing	2–3 per m²/10 sq. ft
Flowering time	Mid–late summer
Hardiness	Zone 7

AMERICAN ORIGIN
This perennial is named after the Mohican *sachem* (chief) Joseph Shauquethqueat, also known as Joe Pye, from Massachusetts.

Eutrochium purpureum

Meadowsweet

Filipendula aka queen of the prairie

European meadowsweet (*F. ulmaria*) is a familiar wild flower of ditches and boggy ground, with its fluffy heads of creamy white flowers. North American *F. rubra* is a taller, more imposing plant with fluffy clouds of attractive pink flowers that bring a touch of softness. The cultivar *F.r.* 'Venusta' is deep rose-pink.

WHERE TO GROW

These are tall plants for an herbaceous border in moist to damp soil. They grow in sun or partial shade among shrubs or other tall perennials.

HOW TO GROW

When planting meadowsweet, add organic matter to the soil to retain moisture, or position it in a damp hollow or at the edge of a pond to ensure the soil doesn't dry out.

GROWING TIP

Cut back the stems in autumn, to prevent them collapsing in windy weather. Plants are easily divided in autumn (see Dividing perennials, page 92).

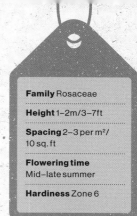

Family Rosaceae

Height 1–2m/3–7ft

Spacing 2–3 per m²/ 10 sq. ft

Flowering time Mid–late summer

Hardiness Zone 6

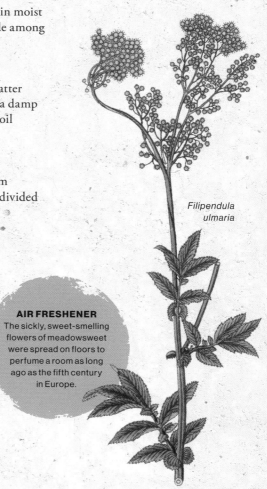

Filipendula ulmaria

Filipendula rubra

AIR FRESHENER
The sickly, sweet-smelling flowers of meadowsweet were spread on floors to perfume a room as long ago as the fifth century in Europe.

Cranesbill

Geranium aka hardy geranium

Cranesbill is consistently one of the most popular
perennials for gardeners, with its bright rounded flowers
in shades of blue, purple, magenta, pink and white.
Different forms can be in flower from spring to autumn.

—

WHERE TO GROW

There are many species and cultivars of *Geranium* but
they generally like moist, free-draining soil, in full sun or
partial shade. *Geranium macrorrhizum* is a great plant for
dry shade. These easy herbaceous border perennials make
mounds of foliage topped by masses of flowers. Some
scramble through a border with long trailing stems.

HOW TO GROW

Cranesbill has explosive seed pods that fire seeds far
and wide, but some hybrids, like *G*. Rozanne, are
sterile and must be propagated from basal cuttings
in summer (see Stem cuttings, page 27).

GROWING TIP

Those cranesbill that flower in early summer,
like *G*. 'Orion' and *G*. 'Brookside', can be cut back
after flowering to encourage a second
flush of bloom.

Family Geraniaceae

Height 25–100cm/
10–39in

Spacing 3–7 per m²/
10 sq. ft

Flowering time
Late spring–autumn

Hardiness Zone 6

Geranium Rozanne

MISTAKEN IDENTITY
The common name geranium
is often used for the popular
indoor plants with the botanical
name *Pelargonium*.

*Geranium
maculatum*

Avens

Geum

These pretty, low-growing perennials have thin branched stems holding small rounded flowers like miniature single roses, to which they are related. Flower colours range from deep red to pink, orange and yellow.

—

WHERE TO GROW
The soil for avens should be moisture-retentive but not waterlogged. They do well in full sun or partial shade but flowering is often better with more sunshine. They do not like a hot and dry position.

HOW TO GROW
Avens forms a semi-evergreen rosette of leaves that can be crowded out by nearby plants. They are best positioned near the front of a border but the flower stems of taller forms, like *G.* 'Totally Tangerine', will reach above surrounding plants.

GROWING TIP
After growing for a few years, plants can be divided in autumn or spring, to give them more space and encourage better flowering (see Dividing perennials, page 92).

Family Rosaceae	
Height 25–100cm/ 10–39in	
Spacing 7–9 per m²/ 10 sq. ft	
Flowering time Late spring–midsummer	
Hardiness Zone 7	

Geum 'Totally Tangerine'

WET FEET
Water avens (*Geum rivale*) is a plant of damp ground and waterside locations in Europe and North America.

Geum coccineum

Using colour in a border

It is the flower colour of perennials that have the greatest impact. A border can be themed around a single colour or group of colours. A famous example is the White Garden at Sissinghurst in Kent, UK, but with so many colours to choose from it seems a shame to restrict yourself to just one.

Colours create a mood. Pastel shades, such as pale pink, mauve, pale blue and yellow, have a subtle soothing effect. For a pastel theme, look at bellflowers (*Campanula*), yarrows like *Achillea* 'Moonshine', irises, cranesbill (*Geranium*), masterwort (*Astrantia*) and blue star (*Amsonia*).

In contrast, bright reds, oranges and magenta can be brash and dramatic. For a 'hot' border, try sneezeweed (*Helenium*), penstemons, red lobelias, red-hot poker (*Kniphofia*) and some of the deeper-coloured day lilies (*Hemerocallis*).

Not all colours go well together so, to help with plant associations, have a look at the colour wheel. Colours on opposite sides of the colour wheel are complementary and look good together, such as orange and blue or yellow and violet. Colours next to each other on the wheel look harmonious so lack contrast; add a third colour to bring the combination to life.

There are no strict rules and everyone has different tastes, so experiment. There are numerous shades of each colour, and some will work better than others. For example, pink can be very pale to deep magenta. The final effect will depend on which shade you choose. You can also add a scattering of strongly coloured flowers to a pastel scheme to catch your eye, like the magenta *Silene coronaria*. And don't forget silvery foliage or white flowers, which go with almost anything.

A A simple colour wheel has three main colours – red, yellow and blue – plus intermediate ones.

B The pastel colours of the yarrow, purple coneflower (*Echinacea*), purple loosestrife (*Lythrum*) and mulleins (*Verbascum*) create a soothing palette.

C The deep orange or red of sneezeweeds like *Helenium* 'Rubinzwerg' provide warm russet tones in a late summer border.

D *Geum* 'Totally Tangerine' and blue star (*Amsonia tabernaemontana*) are complementary colours, opposite each other on the colour wheel.

E Yellow *Achillea filipendulina* 'Gold Plate' and pink *Filipendula rubra* 'Venusta' have complementary colours that go well together.

Gypsophila

Gypsophila aka baby's breath

Billowing clouds of small white flowers on a tangle of wiry branched stems are sent up by *G. paniculata* – a plant beloved by flower arrangers. Other perennial species include low-growing, creeping *G. repens* and alpine *G. cerastioides*.

—

WHERE TO GROW
Gypsophila likes alkaline to neutral, well-drained soil. Mix it with a variety of other plants in a sunny herbaceous border or grow it in a dry garden.

HOW TO GROW
This plant likes alkaline to neutral, well-drained soil. Add grit to heavy soil to improve drainage. *Gypsophila repens* is best at the front of a border, where the glaucous leaves will bring contrasting foliage colour, while more upright plants thread their way through the airy panicles. *Gypsophila cerastioides* is great for containers.

GROWING TIP
Perennial gypsophilas resent being disturbed so it best to grow them from seed sown in late winter (see Growing from seed, page 25) or take side shoots as basal shoot cuttings in late summer (see Stem cuttings, page 27).

Family Caryophyllaceae	
Height 10–120cm/ 4–48in	
Spacing 2–3 per m²/ 10 sq. ft	
Flowering time Early–midsummer	
Hardiness Zone 6–7	

Gypsophila paniculata

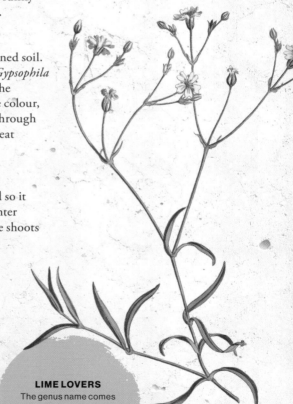

LIME LOVERS
The genus name comes from *Gypsos*, meaning gypsum, and *philos*, which means loving.

Gypsophila repens

Sneezeweed

Helenium aka sneezewort, Helen's flower

The North American sneezeweeds are valued for late summer colour, when they produce a profusion of daisy-like flowers. Their petals are usually three-lobed and surround a prominent rounded cone of tiny disc florets.

—

WHERE TO GROW

A sunny border with moist, free-draining soil is perfect for sneezeweeds, as is prairie-style planting with grasses (see Mixing perennials with grasses, page 118), but they are not particularly drought tolerant.

HOW TO GROW

Plant in clusters to highlight the bright yellow, orange or deep rusty red blooms. Some sneezeweeds flower from midsummer, like *H.* 'Sahin's Early Flowerer', while others, including *H.* 'Waltraut' and *H.* 'Moerheim Beauty', will extend the season into autumn. Propagate by division after flowering or in spring (see page 92).

GROWING TIP

Sneezeweed can fall over in windy weather, especially if planted in partial shade, where they are likely to grow taller. Stake plants to hold them up, or mix them with other tall perennials so they support each other.

Helenium 'Sahin's Early Flowerer'

Family Asteraceae	
Height 45–125cm/ 18–50in	
Spacing 5–7 per m²/ 10 sq. ft	
Flowering time Midsummer–autumn	
Hardiness Zone 7	

Helenium autumnale

TAKE A SNIFF
Dried *Helenium* used to be inhaled through the nose by native Americans, like snuff, and this is reflected in the common name sneezeweed.

Sunflower

Helianthus aka perennial sunflower

Big yellow daisies on tall stems typify sunflowers, especially the annual common sunflower (*H. annuus*). Perennial sunflowers have smaller blooms but can be almost as tall and come back every year, making impressive clumps of late summer colour.

—

WHERE TO GROW

Plant in free-draining but moisture-retentive soil that doesn't dry out in summer. Sunflowers need sun and warmth to flower well so grow them in a south- or west-facing herbaceous border or against a sunny wall (see Planting tall perennials to add height, page 128).

HOW TO GROW

Helianthus 'Lemon Queen' is a particularly good form, loved by butterflies, and *H. salicifolius* is worth growing for its long narrow leaves. These tall plants need room to grow, and their stems may require support.

GROWING TIP

Propagate sunflowers by division in autumn (see Dividing perennials, page 92) or from seed sown in spring (see Growing from seed, page 25). Division can also reinvigorate established clumps.

Family Asteraceae

Height 1–2m/3–7ft

Spacing 2–3 per m²/ 10 sq. ft

Flowering time Mid–late summer

Hardiness Zone 4–5

Helianthus 'Lemon Queen'

ROOT VEG
Helianthus tuberosus is the Jerusalem artichoke, grown for its edible knobbly tubers.

Helianthus giganteus

Hellebore

Helleborus aka Christmas rose, lenten rose

Hellebores are among the first perennials to appear as winter comes to an end. Flowers vary from green hanging bells to rounded, outward-facing blooms in shades of pink, purple and white, sometimes attractively speckled.

—

Family Ranunculaceae	
Height 30–90cm/ 12–36in	
Spacing 5–7 per m²/ 10 sq. ft	
Flowering time Winter–spring	
Hardiness Zone 7	

WHERE TO GROW

Plant hellebores in a shady woodland bed or partially shaded herbaceous border, where they are protected from drought and hot summer sun. The soil should be humus-rich and moisture-retentive. See also Using perennials in a winter garden, page 46.

HOW TO GROW

The leaves can become untidy so cut off the old foliage from the base, as new shoots emerge. Some species, including *H. argutifolius* and *H. foetidus*, have stout leafy stems. Remove their flower heads once they have faded, to encourage more basal growth.

GROWING TIP

Divide clump-forming hellebores in autumn (see Dividing perennials, page 92). Sow seed as fresh as possible in spring, still green and straight from the seed pod (see Growing from seed, page 25).

Helleborus foetidus

NOT A ROSE
Despite the common names Christmas rose and Lenten rose, these plants are unrelated to roses, but their names do reflect their flowering time.

Helleborus niger

Day lily

Hemerocallis

The colourful, trumpet-shaped flowers of day lilies are produced on stiff branching stems above a fountain of long, strap-like leaves. Although the flowers last only a day, they are produced consecutively over several weeks.

—

WHERE TO GROW

Day lilies are tough plants, growing in a range of conditions but a sunny herbaceous border is ideal. In shade, flowering will reduce. They can be grown in poor soils and will survive drought conditions, although they may stop flowering. They are best in moisture-retentive, free-draining soil.

HOW TO GROW

The bright flowers make day lilies a great addition to a strong colour scheme or hot border (see Using colour in a border, page 74), but some forms can become a nuisance, spreading through a bed untamed.

GROWING TIP

Their roaming nature means day lilies naturally spread so you may not need to propagate them, but forms that remain in compact clumps are easy to divide in spring or autumn (see Dividing perennials, page 92).

Family Asphodelaceae

Height 60–120cm/ 24–48in

Spacing 3–5 per m²/ 10 sq. ft

Flowering time Early–midsummer

Hardiness Zone 6

Hemerocallis 'Bonanza'

DAILY SNACK
The young buds of some day lilies can be eaten off the plant. They have a peppery taste.

Hemerocallis fulva

Coral bells

Heuchera

Coral bells are mostly grown for their low mounds of colourful, patterned, evergreen leaves, often in vibrant colours. The flowers are small but numerous, and are held on upright racemes above the foliage.

WHERE TO GROW

These easy ground-cover plants do best in partial or full shade, as long as the soil isn't permanently wet. Plant at the front of a border or filling the gaps between other plants. Coral bells also make excellent container plants (see Planting a container with perennials, page 82). See also Planting perennials for foliage, page 38.

HOW TO GROW

The leaf colours can be bold, which makes coral bells hard to combine with other plants, but they look great when displayed in a pot or window box. Propagate by division in autumn (see Dividing perennials, page 92).

GROWING TIP

Coral bells can be grown in full sun if the soil retains some moisture, but their leaves can be scorched in hot weather, especially the pale colour forms.

Family Saxifragaceae	
Height 30–45cm/ 12–18in	
Spacing 7–9 per m²/ 10 sq. ft	
Flowering time Early–midsummer	
Hardiness Zone 6	

Heuchera sanguinea

BEST OF BOTH
Coral bells and foam flower (*Tiarella*) have been crossed to make × *Heucherella*, which has patterned leaves and foamy flower heads.

Leaf colours of coral bells

Planting a container with perennials

Many perennials can be grown in a container, either as an individual specimen in a pot, or grouped together in a window box or large planter. They can make a seasonal flower display or look good year-round. Evergreen perennials with attractive foliage, like coral bells (*Heuchera*), are useful for year-round interest.

Once you have chosen what plant, or plants, you want to grow, you need to find a suitable container. If it is too small, the plants will quickly outgrow the space and the display will look top-heavy. If the container is too large, the plants will look disproportionately small. Small containers will also need watering more frequently, and there is a risk that the soil will dry out completely in hot weather.

The container should have holes in the bottom, to allow excess water to drain away. Cover these holes with pieces of old terracotta pots, stones or a piece of mesh. This should allow the water through but stop the soil falling out. Then fill the container with loam-based potting soil and arrange your plants. The recommended spacing for plants in a garden border can be ignored. Plant close together for a more immediate effect, but remember how big each plant is likely to get and allow some room for growth.

Water well after planting, until water drains out of the holes in the bottom. This can make the pot heavy so it is a good idea to move it to its final location, such as a patio, terrace or front doorstep, before watering. Then sit back and enjoy the display.

1. Choose your plants and a suitable container. These are two coral bells, × *Heucherella* 'Stoplight' and *Heuchera* 'Timeless Treasure', plus hardy plumbago (*Ceratostigma plumbaginoides*).
2. Once you have covered the drainage holes, fill the container with loam-based potting soil to about two-thirds of its depth, leaving room for the root balls of the plants.
3. Remove the plants from their pots and place them on the soil so that the base of the plant (top of the root ball) is just below the rim of the container.
4. Fill in the gaps around the plants with more of the soil mix and firm it down. Then top up the soil so that the final level is the same as the base of the plants. If the plants are too deep they can rot, and if positioned too high they can dry out quickly.
5. Once planted, your container is ready to move to its chosen spot in the garden. Then give it plenty of water to ensure all the soil is moist.

Hosta

Hosta aka plantain lily

These are among the best foliage plants, with their broad leaves in all shades of green, often prominently ribbed and sometimes variegated. Flowers are narrow and lily-like, appearing in summer.

WHERE TO GROW

Miniature hostas are best in a pot, while the larger forms, with their wide sumptuous leaves, grow best in humus-rich, moist soil in a woodland bed or herbaceous border, in partial or full shade. They also make great container plants (see Planting a container with perennials, page 82).

HOW TO GROW

Hostas are notoriously susceptible to slug and snail damage. To avoid using chemical controls, pick them off as soon as you see them, use deterrents like sharp grit around the plants, or grow large vigorous clumps so the damage is less obvious.

GROWING TIP

Divide hostas in early spring (see Dividing perennials, page 92). They can be split into individual growing points, each with some root attached, to make many new plants.

Family Asparagaceae

Height 30–90cm/ 12–36in

Spacing 5–7 per m²/ 10 sq. ft

Flowering time Early–midsummer

Hardiness Zone 7

Hosta 'Liberty'

FEEDING TIME
It isn't only slugs and snails that enjoy hostas; humans have been known to eat the leaves, once boiled like cabbage, and the shoots once roasted.

Hosta sieboldiana

Ice plant

Hylotelephium aka *Sedum*, orpine

These succulent herbaceous perennials have fleshy rounded leaves that can be green, pale blue-green or purplish. Flowers are small and star-like, and are densely packed in domed or flat heads from late summer.

—

WHERE TO GROW

Ice plants are best grown in a sunny herbaceous border or dry garden. Their late summer flowers combine well with shorter grasses (see Mixing perennials with grasses, page 118). They tolerate some shade but may become weak, with fewer flowers. Plant in free-draining soil; add organic matter to heavy soil to improve drainage.

HOW TO GROW

These succulent perennials tolerate of a range of conditions except ground that remains wet all winter. Once established, ice plants can survive long periods of drought. Propagate from cuttings taken in early summer (see Taking stem cuttings to get more plants, page 102) or by division in spring (see Dividing perennials, page 92).

GROWING TIP

After flowering, leave the stems to provide some structural interest in a winter border. Cut them back as new shoots emerge in early spring (see Delay cutting back perennials, page 108).

Hylotelephium telephium

Family	Crassulaceae
Height	30–60cm/ 12–24in
Spacing	5–7 per m²/ 10 sq. ft
Flowering time	Late summer–autumn
Hardiness	Zone 7

SEDUM TO YOU
Ice plants were long known as *Sedum* but are now in their own genus, *Hylotelephium*.

Hylotelephium spectabile

Inula

Inula

Inulas have yellow daisy flowers, often with numerous, very narrow petals on their ray florets, making distinctive inflorescences. They are leafy plants that can reach 2m/7ft tall in some species.

—

WHERE TO GROW

Grow inulas in fertile, moisture-retentive but free-draining soil. They do best in a sunny herbaceous border but can be planted in partial shade. They will not tolerate drought.

HOW TO GROW

Some, like *I. magnifica*, can add height to a border and have huge leaves (see Planting tall perennials to add height, page 128), but the more compact species, like *I. hookeri*, are often more floriferous. Propagate by division in spring or autumn (see Dividing perennials, page 92), or from seed sown in spring (see Growing from seed, page 25).

GROWING TIP

The leaves of *I. magnifica* can slowly spread, its big leaves swamping other plants, so reduce clumps of this perennial every few years. Deadheading can encourage a second flush of bloom.

Family	Asteraceae
Height	0.6–2m/2–7ft
Spacing	3–5 per m²/ 10 sq. ft
Flowering time	Mid–late summer
Hardiness	Zone 6

Inula helenium

Inula hookeri

ANCIENT HISTORY
Elecampane (*Inula helenium*) has a long history of medicinal use, going as far back as the Ancient Greeks.

Iris

Iris aka bearded iris, flag iris, Siberian iris, water iris

There are many different irises, from small bulbs to those with thick rhizomes and fans of pointed leaves. They all have easily recognizable flowers, with three upright standards and three arching falls, in a range of glorious colours.

WHERE TO GROW

Irises grow in a variety of conditions. Plant water-loving species, like *I. ensata* and *I. pseudacorus*, in damp boggy ground. Those with thick rhizomes, including the bearded irises, should be planted in well-drained soil and full sun. Others, like the Siberian irises, prefer a partially shaded herbaceous border or woodland garden.

HOW TO GROW

Although their flowers may last only a week or two, iris leaves add contrasting shapes and textures to a planting scheme. All irises can be increased by division in spring or late summer (see Dividing perennials, page 92).

GROWING TIP

Plant irises with thick rhizomes on the soil surface, to prevent rotting. Peg them down with a wire loop pushed in the ground until their roots have grown into the soil.

Family Iridaceae	
Height 20–120cm/ 8–48in	
Spacing 7–9 per m²/ 10 sq. ft	
Flowering time Spring–midsummer	
Hardiness Zone 6	

Iris spuria

Iris pseudacorus

RAINBOW COLOURS
Iris is named after the Greek goddess of the rainbow, as its flowers come in many colours.

Scabious

Knautia aka field scabious, Macedonian scabious

The dark purple to crimson, pincushion flowers of Macedonian scabious (*K. macedonica*) are small but they appear over several weeks. They are held on thin branching stems, above the tuft of lobed basal leaves. Field scabious (*K. arvensis*) has lilac-purple flowers.
—

WHERE TO GROW

These plants need plenty of sunshine and free-draining soil; and prefer it to be neutral to alkaline. Grow in an herbaceous border or in a flower meadow.

HOW TO GROW

Both Macedonian and field scabious are great mixers. When planted in a border, the spindly stems will mingle with other plants, pushing their crimson or lilac-purple flowers above the surrounding leaves. Without surrounding plants, they can become floppy and so need support.

GROWING TIP

Scabious will seed around by itself, but you can sow seed in early spring (see Growing from seed, page 25). Take cuttings from basal shoots in spring (see Stem cuttings, page 27).

Family Caprifoliaceae

Height 40–120cm/ 16–48in

Spacing 5–7 per m²/ 10 sq. ft

Flowering time Early–late summer

Hardiness Zone 7

HISTORIC ROOTS
Macedonia is a region of Europe now covered by several Balkan countries including Bulgaria, North Macedonia and parts of Greece.

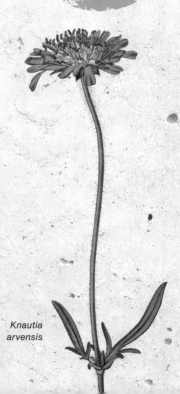

Knautia arvensis

Knautia arvensis

Red-hot poker

Kniphofia aka torch lily

Despite the common name, the flowers on red-hot pokers aren't always red – there are also other hot colours including orange and yellow, as well as white. The narrow tubular blooms form a dense elongated cluster on stiff upright stems, above narrow arching leaves.

—

WHERE TO GROW
Plant red-hot pokers in moist but free-draining soil. They will survive drought and need sun to flower well. These exotic-looking perennials do best in a hot border or gravel garden (see Making a gravel garden, page 68). Shorter forms can be grown at the front of a border or in a container (see Planting a container with perennials, page 82).

HOW TO GROW
The leaves of some, like *K. caulescens*, have an architectural quality that make a statement in a border and the tallest red-hot pokers can reach nearly 2m/7ft. Shorter forms, like *K.* Popsicle Series, are only 60cm/24in tall.

GROWING TIP
The smaller forms, with grassy leaves, are easiest to divide, in early spring, while the larger forms will need cutting apart, using a sharp knife to slice through the rhizomes (see Dividing perennials, page 92).

Family Asphodelaceae

Height 0.6–2m/2–7ft

Spacing 2–5 per m²/ 10 sq. ft

Flowering time Midsummer–autumn

Hardiness Zone 5

OUT OF AFRICA
Almost all red-hot pokers are from Africa, but they are grown in temperate gardens around the world.

Kniphofia rooperi

Kniphofia caulescens

Bleeding heart

Lamprocapnos spectabilis aka *Dicentra spectabilis,* Dutchman's breeches, locks and keys

A single species, *L. spectabilis,* that was previously included in *Dicentra,* has been moved to its own genus. It is a spring garden highlight. Long arching stems hold a string of pendent blooms, each one heart-shaped with protruding inner petals.

—

WHERE TO GROW

Bleeding heart can be grown in sun or partial shade, in a border or woodland garden, as long as the soil retains moisture. Plant in fertile, humus-rich soil, around shrubs or deciduous trees.

HOW TO GROW

This herbaceous perennial looks great flowering with bulbs like grape hyacinths (*Muscari*) and late daffodils, and the white form, *L.s.* 'Alba', has a purity that combines beautifully with white tulips. Divide plants after flowering, but be careful as they are delicate (see Dividing perennials, page 92). Take root cuttings in winter (see Root cuttings, page 28).

GROWING TIP

The spring flowers of bleeding heart bring early colour to a border, but the gap they leave after flowering needs to be hidden by surrounding them with summer perennials.

Family Papaveraceae

Height 50–70cm/ 20–28in

Spacing 5–7 per m²/ 10 sq. ft

Flowering time Spring–early summer

Hardiness Zone 6

LEAF ALONE
The foliage of bleeding heart can be an irritant and prove poisonous if ingested raw, causing confusion, dizziness and irritability.

Lamprocapnos spectabilis

Lamprocapnos spectabilis

Blazing star

Liatris aka button snakewort, gayfeather

Above long narrow leaves rise the feathery spikes of
blazing star, which comprise many densely packed
clusters of small starry flowers. The blooms are usually
pink or purple, but white forms are also available.

—

WHERE TO GROW

Grow blazing star in full sun in an herbaceous
border. It mixes well with grasses and other flowering
perennials, scattered through a naturalistic planting
scheme (see Naturalistic planting, page 17). The soil
should be free-draining but moisture-retentive, never
drying out completely or becoming waterlogged in
winter.

HOW TO GROW

Blazing star typically flowers in the second half of
summer, bringing some late season colour to a border.
Liatris spicata is the most commonly grown species in
gardens, where it reaches about 70cm/28in but some
like *L. pycnostachya* are taller, growing to 1.5m/5ft.

GROWING TIP

Propagate by division in spring (see Dividing
perennials, page 92) to spread your plants around.
They look best mingling with other perennials
instead of planted in large groups.

Liatris spicata

Family	Asteraceae
Height	0.6–1.5m/2–5ft
Spacing	4–5 per m²/ 10 sq. ft
Flowering time	Mid–late summer
Hardiness	Zone 7

EASY GROWER
Liatris grows from a corm or
small rhizome, which can be
planted like a summer bulb.

*Liatris
spicata*

Dividing perennials

Division is a simple way to increase any clump-forming or spreading plant that has several growing points. It usually requires lifting the plant out of the ground and cutting the root ball into pieces, and therefore should be done when the plant is dormant, from late autumn to early spring.

At the end of summer, don't cut back the dry stems of plants that you want to divide, so you can easily locate them in winter and assess the extent of their spread. If you have several plants you want to divide, you can mark them with a bamboo cane to help you remember where they are.

When the time comes to divide the plant, cut off the old stems. By late winter, new shoots may already be starting to grow so be careful not to damage them too much when you split the clump at that time of year. Dig around the plant to loosen the soil and free the roots, then use a garden fork to slowly lift it out of the ground. Once removed, place the clump on the ground and cut it into pieces. This can be done with a spade pushed through the clump from top to bottom to split it, or with a pair of garden forks pushed into the clump back to back and then eased apart to split the root ball. The divisions can be split again to make more new plants – but don't be too greedy. You want strong divisions with plenty of roots that will quickly re-establish once planted. See also Division, page 28.

1 Cut back old stems on the plant you want to divide. If there are new shoots, be careful not to damage them.
2 Loosen the soil around the plant and dig down to expose the edge of the root ball.
3 Use a garden fork to gently lift the plant out of the soil.
4 Then place the plant back on the ground and cut through it with a spade to split the root ball in two.
5 The divisions can be split again and the pieces removed to be planted nearby to make a bigger group, or be moved elsewhere in the garden.
6 Replant each division and firm the soil. Give some water to settle it in.

Leopard plant

Ligularia

These are stately plants with large leaves and bright orange-yellow daisy flowers. The flowers are usually held in broad heads above the foliage, but in some leopard plants, like the popular *L.* 'The Rocket', they are on dramatic spires.

WHERE TO GROW

Grow in damp soil, by a pond or stream, in a woodland garden or partially shaded border.

HOW TO GROW

Leopard plants must have moisture in the soil all year round. Hot sun can cause them to wilt or scorch the leaves but they will tolerate some sunshine if the soil isn't dry. They can also be damaged by strong winds so some shelter is beneficial. Propagate by division in spring or late summer (see Dividing perennials, page 92).

GROWING TIP

These can be large plants so give them room to grow and display their attractive, dark green leaves, which are a feature on their own.

Family Asteraceae

Height 1–1.8m/3–6ft

Spacing 2–3 per m²/ 10 sq. ft

Flowering time Mid–late summer

Hardiness Zone 6

CHANGING SPOTS

The name 'leopard plant' comes from the spotted leaves of a species now in a different genus – *Farfugium japonicum*.

Ligularia dentata

Ligularia stenocephala

Lobelia

Lobelia aka cardinal flower, devil's tobacco

The hardy perennial lobelias are striking plants, with vivid flower colours, including the bright scarlet cardinal flower (*L. cardinalis*). The individual blooms are held on upright spikes.

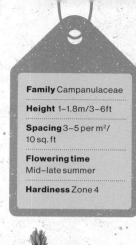

Family Campanulaceae	
Height 1–1.8m/3–6ft	
Spacing 3–5 per m²/ 10 sq. ft	
Flowering time Mid–late summer	
Hardiness Zone 4	

WHERE TO GROW

The cardinal flower needs damp ground, near a pond or stream, while the exotic-looking devil's tobacco (*L. tupa*) can be grown in a sunny herbaceous border.

HOW TO GROW

Hardy lobelias will survive a frost but can die in a harsh winter. Cut them back and apply a thick mulch, 10cm/4in deep, over the crown to protect from the cold. They are more likely to survive in a sheltered location, a town garden or along the coast, where temperatures are milder. Propagate from seed sown in spring (see Growing from seed, page 25).

GROWING TIP

The blue, white or purple trailing lobelia often seen in hanging baskets, pots and bedding displays is a tender perennial, normally grown from seed every year.

Lobelia cardinalis

TROPICAL ALPINES
There are over 400 species of *Lobelia*, including giant lobelias that grow high on equatorial mountains.

Lobelia tupa

Lupin

Lupinus aka lupine

Lupin is a cottage-garden favourite that flowers from early summer. The pea flowers are held on tall spires and come in an assortment of bold and bright colours. The distinctive leaves are palmately divided. All parts are poisonous.

—

WHERE TO GROW

Plant lupins in a sunny position in a mixed or herbaceous border, ideally in neutral to acidic soil, informally positioned or in broad colourful groups. They will tolerate partial shade. They can also be grown in poor soils but can rot in damp ground over winter.

HOW TO GROW

Make sure your lupins have some sun as too much shade will cause them to grow weakly and eventually collapse without some staking. Propagate from basal cuttings in spring (see Stem cuttings, page 27).

GROWING TIP

Lupin aphids (see Cultivation and physical techniques, page 135) can quickly smother a plant so as soon as you see them remove and dispose of the leaves and shoots that have been affected.

Family	Fabaceae
Height	45–150cm/ 18–60in
Spacing	3–5 per m²/ 10 sq. ft
Flowering time	Early–midsummer
Hardiness	Zone 5

Mixed lupin cultivars

GETTING A FIX
Lupins have nitrogen-fixing bacteria in their roots, enabling them to grow in nutrient-poor soil.

Lupinus luteus

Yellow loosestrife

Lysimachia aka creeping Jenny, garden loosestrife, golden candles

Yellow loosestrife usually forms spreading clumps, with masses of golden yellow, occasionally white, flowers on upright stems. The cup-shaped flowers are held in the upper leaf axils or in clusters at the end of the stem.

—

WHERE TO GROW

Plant yellow loosestrife in full sun or partial shade by a pond or stream where the soil is damp. It can also be grown in moist soil in an herbaceous border.

HOW TO GROW

Add organic matter to the soil when planting, to improve moisture retention. Plants spread by rhizomatous roots and are easily increased by division in spring or autumn (see Dividing perennials, page 92).

GROWING TIP

Creeping Jenny (*L. nummularia*) is a vigorous, evergreen, ground-hugging plant that is useful for covering the soil in a border or container.

Family Primulaceae	
Height 10–120cm/ 4–48in	
Spacing 5–7 per m²/ 10 sq. ft	
Flowering time Midsummer	
Hardiness Zone 6	

Lysimachia verticillaris

CALM DOWN
The common name means to 'lose strife', and plants are said to have a calming effect.

Lysimachia vulgaris

Purple loosestrife

Lythrum aka wand loosestrife

Purple loosestrife is an attractive border perennial with
densely packed spikes of purple to rosy pink flowers
held on upright or gently waving stems. Two commonly
grown species are *L. salicaria* and *L. virgatum*, which
have several cultivars worth trying.

—

WHERE TO GROW
Although completely unrelated to yellow loosestrife
(*Lysimachia*: see page 97), purple loosestrife needs
similar cultural conditions so grow in moist soil in
a border or around the edge of a pond. Plant in a
sunny position where purple loosestrife can make an
impressive stand of tall flowering stems.

HOW TO GROW
Propagate by division in autumn or early spring (see
Dividing perennials, page 92), or sow seed in winter (see
Growing from seed, page 25).

GROWING TIP
When growing purple loosestrife in shallow water
around the edge of a pond, plant it in a mesh basket
to restrict its spread.

Family Lythraceae	
Height 60–120cm/ 24–48in	
Spacing 4–6 per m²/ 10 sq. ft	
Flowering time Mid–late summer	
Hardiness Zone 7	

UNWELCOME VISITOR
Native to Eurasia, *L. salicaria*
has invaded almost every
state of the USA, where it is a
problem weed.

Lythrum salicaria

Lythrum
salicaria

Plume poppy

Macleaya

These architectural plants are valued as much for their foliage as for the sprays of tiny, buff to whitish flowers at the top of tall stems. The large scalloped leaves are blue-green with whitish undersides.

—

WHERE TO GROW

Plume poppy is tolerant of a range of soils and makes a handsome feature in an herbaceous border. (See also Planting tall perennials to add height, page 128.) It is best in moist but well-drained soil in sun or partial shade.

HOW TO GROW

Plants can spread rapidly in fertile soil if left unchecked. Stems are easy to remove, but make sure this is done regularly to prevent plume poppy getting out of control. It is worth the effort for the wonderful foliage.

GROWING TIP

If you need to increase your stock or introduce it to another part of the garden, separate sections at the edge of the clump in spring or autumn (see Dividing perennials, page 92).

Family	Papaveraceae
Height	1.5–2.5m/5–8ft
Spacing	2–3 per m²/ 10 sq. ft
Flowering time	Midsummer
Hardiness	Zone 6

Macleaya cordata

Macleaya cordata

CLOSE RELATIONS
Plume poppy looks very different to the common poppy (*Papaver*),] but they are in the same plant family.

Bergamot

Monarda aka bee balm

Leafy stems hold up compact terminal heads comprising whorls of two-lipped flowers. Their colours range from white and pink to purple and red. They are particularly attractive to bees. The foliage is aromatic, giving off a spicy fragrance when crushed.

—

WHERE TO GROW

Bergamot needs a sunny position to flower well but does grow in partial shade. Plant in moist but well-drained soil in a mixed or herbaceous border. Avoid waterlogged soil. Bergamot complements Mediterranean-style planting but isn't especially drought tolerant.

HOW TO GROW

Most bergamots grow to about 1m/3ft tall, but shorter forms are available that can be placed nearer the front of a border. Propagate by division in early spring (see Dividing perennials, page 92) or by taking cuttings of basal shoots (see Stem cuttings, page 27).

GROWING TIP

All bergamots are susceptible to powdery mildew in hot dry weather. Hide by planting behind shorter perennials or look for mildew-resistant forms; however, none is immune.

Family	Lamiaceae
Height	45–100cm/ 18–39in
Spacing	3–5 per m²/ 10 sq. ft
Flowering time	Mid–late summer
Hardiness	Zone 4–5

Monarda didyma

Monarda didyma Balmy Purple

CITRUS SCENT
The essential oil in the leaves has a similar fragrance to bergamot orange – hence the common name.

Catmint

Nepeta aka catnip, garden catmint

Masses of usually blue or violet flowers are borne over a long period in summer on this easy, reliable perennial. The flowers are held in spikes above the often grey-green, aromatic leaves.

—

WHERE TO GROW
Catmint needs plenty of sunshine to flower well and should be grown in well-drained soil. Taller forms make large clumps in an herbaceous border or a gravel garden (see Making a gravel garden, page 68) and low-growing forms can be planted to spill over the edges of paths.

HOW TO GROW
Trim spent flower spikes, to encourage new flowering stems. By late summer the main stems become woody so cut them right back in autumn, to allow space for the new shoots.

GROWING TIP
Taking softwood cuttings in summer, from leafy, non-flowering shoots, is an easy way to propagate catmints (see Taking stem cuttings to get more plants, page 102). They can also be divided in spring or autumn (see Dividing perennials, page 92).

Nepeta 'Six Hills Giant'

Family	Lamiaceae
Height	30–90cm/ 12–36in
Spacing	3–5 per m²/ 10 sq. ft
Flowering time	Mid–late summer
Hardiness	Zone 6–7

LOVE/HATE
The smell of catmint is extremely attractive to cats, but humans can use it as an insect repellent.

Nepeta cataria

Taking stem cuttings to get more plants

Taking cuttings is one of the easiest ways to propagate many perennials. All you need is a knife or a pair of secateurs, a pot of cutting soil mix and somewhere sheltered to keep the pot while the cuttings grow roots. This can be a cold frame or a cool greenhouse if you have one, or a windowsill that isn't too hot and sunny.

Cut young, healthy, non-flowering stems, taken from new growth or after flowering at the end of summer. A plant like catmint (*Nepeta*) will grow shoots all summer but avoid taking cuttings on a hot sunny day, as the plants will be stressed. Wait for a cooler cloudy day or take the cuttings early in the morning. It is not unusual for some cuttings to fail so, to be sure, take about twice as many as you want.

Remove most of the leaves from your cuttings, just keeping a few at the tip, as they lose moisture through any remaining foliage. Then cut the base of each stem just below a node (where the leaves joined the stem and where the new roots will develop). Each cutting should be 7–10cm/3–4in long.

If your cuttings are slow to root, you could try applying hormone rooting powder to the cut end. Perennials that root easily include catmint, sage (*Salvia*) and penstemon, and these are unlikely to need rooting powder. See also Stem cuttings (page 27).

1 Cut a selection of young healthy shoots (here, catmint), and keep them in a bag to prevent them drying out.
2 Remove the lower leaves of each cutting using a sharp knife or your fingers.
3 Cut the stem just below a leaf node, and dip in rooting powder if needed.
4 Fill a pot with cutting soil mix and make a hole for each cutting with a dibber or pencil. Insert the cutting and firm the soil.
5 When the pot is full, water thoroughly to ensure all the soil is moist. Place in a sheltered spot, out of direct sunlight. You can cover the pot with a plastic bag to reduce water loss but most cuttings of perennials don't need this.
6 After a few weeks the cuttings will have rooted. Gently separate them and pot them up individually to grow on before planting out.

Peony

Paeonia

Peony flowers may be fleeting but they are so large and colourful that they should be grown in every garden. The blooms are either single and bowl-shaped or sumptuous doubles, held above attractive divided leaves.

—

WHERE TO GROW
Herbaceous peonies do best in full sun and fertile, moisture-retentive but free-draining soil. They are slow growing but will gradually make broad clumps with long thick roots.

HOW TO GROW
Peonies provide early summer colour in an herbaceous border; mix with plants that will take over the display once the flowers have faded. Propagate by division in autumn as the leaves die back but be sure to dig deep to avoid root damage (see Dividing perennials, page 92).

GROWING TIP
In autumn, cut back the leaves of herbaceous peonies, being careful to avoid any emerging new shoots.

Family Paeoniaceae	
Height 45–90cm/ 18–36in	
Spacing 2–4 per m²/ 10 sq. ft	
Flowering time Late spring–early summer	
Hardiness Zone 6	

Paeonia lactiflora
double form

Paeonia × festiva 'Rosea Plena'

CROSSOVER
Tree peonies have woody stems. Hybrids between them and herbaceous species are called intersectional peonies.

Poppy

Papaver aka oriental poppy, Welsh poppy

Poppies are annual, biennial or perennial. Of the perennials, the oriental poppy (*Papaver orientale*) is the biggest and showiest, with wide flowers of tissue-paper-like petals. The Welsh poppy (*P. cambricum*) is smaller, with pure yellow blooms.

—

WHERE TO GROW

Plant poppies in fertile, moisture-retentive soil in a sunny herbaceous border or informal, cottage-garden-style planting. Welsh poppy will seed around and appear in unexpected locations.

HOW TO GROW

Poppies flower in late spring and early summer then die back, so fill or conceal the resulting gap with later-flowering plants. They can be divided in spring (see Dividing perennials, page 92), but with established plants this is less likely to be successful, so try propagating from root cuttings in early spring (see Root cuttings, page 28).

GROWING TIP

There are many cultivars of oriental poppies in bold colours, from deep red to scarlet, pink and dusky purple. They can be bought as seed, to sow in early spring.

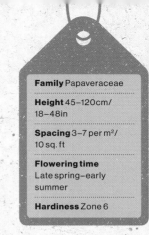

Family Papaveraceae

Height 45–120cm/
18–48in

Spacing 3–7 per m²/
10 sq. ft

Flowering time
Late spring–early
summer

Hardiness Zone 6

Papaver
cambricum

Papaver (Oriental Group) 'Coral Reef'

WELSH OUTLIER
The Welsh poppy used to be in the genus *Meconopsis*, which is best known for Himalayan blue poppies (*M. betonicifolia*).

Patrinia

Patrinia aka eastern valerian, maiden flower

These are clump-forming plants with small, sulphur-yellow flowers in flattish heads on branching inflorescences. The two species usually grown in gardens are the eastern valerian (*P. scabiosifolia*), which is the tallest of this small genus, and maiden flower (*P. triloba*), which is half the height.

—

WHERE TO GROW
The soil for patrinia should be free-draining but hold some moisture. Grow eastern valerian in an open sunny position. Maiden flower is better in a partially shaded border.

HOW TO GROW
Patrinia is easy to propagate from seed sown in late winter (see Growing from seed, page 25), but plants can be also divided in early spring (see Dividing perennials, page 92). Seedlings will flower in their second year.

GROWING TIP
Eastern valerian is best grown as part of a naturalistic-style planting, where its flower heads will intermingle with other plants like purple top (*Verbena bonariensis*; see page 131), burnet (*Sanguisorba*; see page 122) or purple loosestrife (*Lythrum*; see page 98). See also Mixing perennials with grasses, page 118.

Family Caprifoliaceae	
Height 50–100cm/ 20–39in	
Spacing 5–7 per m²/ 10 sq. ft	
Flowering time Mid–late summer	
Hardiness Zone 6	

Patrinia triloba

Patrinia scabiosifolia

PATRIN'S FLEUR
The genus is named after Eugène Patrin, an eighteenth-century French minerologist who also collected plants.

Penstemon

Penstemon aka beardtongue

Among the most colourful and floriferous perennials for the garden are border penstemons, which display racemes of tubular flowers for most of the summer. Leaves are mostly narrow and lance shaped.

—

WHERE TO GROW

Penstemons can be grown in broad swathes in a sunny herbaceous border, cottage-garden-style schemes, in containers or scattered through prairie-style planting (see Mixing perennials with grasses, page 118). Plant in well-drained but moisture-retentive soil. Avoid waterlogged conditions and very exposed sites.

HOW TO GROW

Deadhead to extend the flowering season. Some varieties are less vigorous and short-lived so it is a good idea to take softwood cuttings in summer, to ensure you have plants for the following year (see Taking stem cuttings to get more plants, page 102). Cuttings root easily but need protection over winter.

GROWING TIP

Not all penstemons are fully hardy so wait until spring to tidy them. Then cut them back to their woody base; new shoots will quickly grow.

Penstemon 'Pensham Dorothy Wilson'

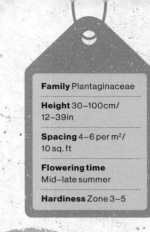

Family Plantaginaceae

Height 30–100cm/ 12–39in

Spacing 4–6 per m²/ 10 sq. ft

Flowering time Mid–late summer

Hardiness Zone 3–5

AMERICAN LIFE
Penstemons are entirely North American, from alpine zones to the subtropics of Guatemala.

Penstemon barbatus

Delay cutting back perennials

When the flowers of perennials have faded, and the stems have dried out, it is tempting to cut them back and tidy the border. There are, however, benefits to leaving them until winter. Their seed heads can look attractive, providing structure and interest, especially on a frosty autumn morning. They are also good for wildlife. Seeds contain protein and fats that are a great food source for birds, voles and mice. Seed heads are also places for insects to shelter and lay their eggs. By removing them early, you are depriving the wildlife in your garden of winter food and shelter.

Visually, the dried stems and seed heads can make an important contribution to the garden in autumn and winter. Some plants retain a structural quality after they have finished flowering. Their stems are robust enough to stand up to wind, rain and light snowfall, and to cut them back early would mean missing out on their architectural value.

Turkish sage (*Phlomis russeliana*) is a good example of a plant that flowers in early summer but retains a presence in the garden right through to winter. It has stiff upright stems and seed heads in whorls. The sturdy dry stems of ice plant (*Hylotelephium*) are robust enough to survive the worst winter weather. Once the stems of perennials start falling over, it is time to cut them back, ready for the new growth to take over. Be careful not to damage new shoots as you cut off the old stems. Once you have tidied the border, mulch it to provide nutrients for the plants for the year ahead.

A Leaving the dried stems and seed heads in a border can result in a wonderful tapestry of textures and forms over autumn and winter, looking especially pretty on a frosty morning.

B The seed heads of Turkish sage create interesting patterns long after they have finished flowering and are most effective when planted in large groups.

C The golden brown, dry flower heads of Culver's root (*Veronicastrum virginicum*) give a warm rustic glow to a border in the autumn sunshine.

D Ice plant has flat-topped flower heads on thick stems that are robust enough to stand up to rough weather right through to late winter.

E When cutting back the dried stems of plants like ice plant (here), be careful not to damage the new season's shoots that will already be starting to grow.

Phlomis

Phlomis aka Jerusalem sage, Turkish sage

Phlomis are typically Mediterranean-climate plants, often shrubby, with grey-green, softly hairy leaves and hooded flowers held in whorls up the stems. Herbaceous species include the wonderful Turkish sage (*P. russeliana*). See also Planting perennials for foliage, page 38.

WHERE TO GROW
Plant phlomis in a sunny position. The shrubby species, like Jerusalem sage (*P. fruticosa*), need well-drained soil and can be grown in a dry garden, and Turkish sage is perfect for an herbaceous border.

HOW TO GROW
Turkish sage forms low clumps of large, roughly hairy, semi-evergreen leaves so needs space to grow. It often doesn't flower the first year after planting, but once established produces tall spikes of pale yellow flowers that dry to form striking seed heads that last into winter (see also Delay cutting back perennials, page 108).

GROWING TIP
Divide Turkish sage in early spring (see Dividing perennials, page 92). Propagate shrubby species from softwood cuttings taken in early summer or semi-ripe cuttings in late summer (see Stem cuttings, page 27).

Phlomis russeliana

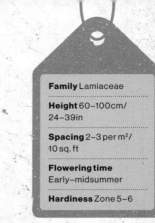

Family Lamiaceae	
Height 60–100cm/ 24–39in	
Spacing 2–3 per m²/ 10 sq. ft	
Flowering time Early–midsummer	
Hardiness Zone 5–6	

EASTERN BRANCH
Several eastern European and Asian species, like *P. tuberosa*, are now in the genus *Phlomoides*.

Phlomis russeliana

Border phlox

Phlox

With their domed heads packed with scented flowers, border phlox have long been popular garden plants. They come in flower colours ranging from pinks and purples to reds, blues and white.

—

WHERE TO GROW

Plant phlox in fertile soil that is moist but never waterlogged. Border phlox are fantastic in a mixed or herbaceous border and are also perfect for a cottage-garden-style planting design, in sun or partial shade.

HOW TO GROW

Their stiff, upright, leafy stems rarely need staking unless in an exposed windy site, but they can be susceptible to powdery mildew in warm sheltered locations. Propagate by division in autumn or early spring (see Dividing perennials, page 92).

GROWING TIP

As with bergamot (*Monarda*; see page 100), if mildew is a problem hide border phlox stems among lower-growing perennials. There are some mildew-resistant varieties worth looking out for.

Family Polemoniaceae

Height 20–150cm/ 8–60in

Spacing 3–5 per m²/ 10 sq. ft

Flowering time Mid–late summer

Hardiness Zone 7

ROCK PHLOX
Alpine species, like *P. subulata*, are great rock garden plants, forming broad mats of spring blooms.

Phlox paniculata

Phlox paniculata 'Eva Cullum'

Obedient plant

Physostegia aka false dragonhead

In this small American genus of plants, there is only one widely grown species, *P. virginiana*, which has several cultivars. The tubular lipped flowers are displayed in vertical ranks around the upright spikes, mostly in a shade of pink, but white forms also occur.

WHERE TO GROW

Plant in full sun or partial shade, in fertile, moisture-retentive soil. Obedient plant can tolerate some drought but is best grown in an herbaceous border where it will form a dense spreading clump of toothed leaves, with multiple flower spikes.

HOW TO GROW

These are late-flowering plants bringing some end-of-season colour to a border, and in the right conditions can spread rapidly. Obedient plant is easy to divide in early spring (see Dividing perennials, page 92) and is largely pest free.

GROWING TIP

Different cultivars vary in height, with some, like *P. virginiana* 'Alba', reaching nearly 1m/3ft tall. Stake these to stop them flopping over.

Family Lamiaceae

Height 45–90cm/ 18–36in

Spacing 5–7 per m²/ 10 sq. ft

Flowering time Late summer–autumn

Hardiness Zone 7

: *Physostegia virginiana* 'Vivid'

WELL-BEHAVED
If you move an individual flower, it will obediently stay in the position you left it.

Physostegia virginiana

Solomon's seal

Polygonatum

These shade-loving perennials grow elegant arching stems bearing pairs or whorls of leaves along their length. The small, bell-shaped flowers hang down from the leaf axils and are often white and green, occasionally mauve.

—

WHERE TO GROW

Plant in fertile, humus-rich soil that isn't waterlogged but never dries out. Solomon's seal needs the shade of a woodland garden or a cool shady border, growing with hostas (see page 84), hellebores (see page 79) and other woodland plants.

HOW TO GROW

The leafy arching stems are a feature, and some, like *P. verticillatum*, have attractive autumn colour as they die down. Cut these stems back in autumn. Propagate these rhizomatous perennials by dividing clumps in early spring (see Dividing perennials, page 92).

GROWING TIP

Solomon's seal is often attacked by polygonatum sawfly. The grey caterpillars defoliate the stems – usually after flowering – so won't kill the plant. Remove the caterpillars as soon as you see them.

Family	Asparagaceae
Height	45–120cm/18–48in
Spacing	5–7 per m²/10 sq. ft
Flowering time	Mid–late spring
Hardiness	Zone 7

Polygonatum odoratum

KNEES UP
Polygonatum means 'many knees' and refers to the many jointed rhizomes.

Polygonatum multiflorum

Cinquefoil

Potentilla aka perennial potentilla, silverweed

Cinquefoils are mostly low-growing herbaceous perennials. They have thin branching stems with saucer-shaped, five-petalled or semi-double flowers, in shades of red, orange or yellow, held above tufts of toothed, strawberry-plant-like leaves.

—

WHERE TO GROW

Most cinquefoils like a sunny position and well-drained soil, while a few, like *P. atrosanguinea*, can be grown in partial shade and are good for ground cover under other plants. Plant along the front of a border, in a cottage-garden-style scheme or as underplanting for shrubs, like roses (*Rosa*).

HOW TO GROW

Remove the flower stems once flowering is over, to encourage more to grow. Divide these clump-forming perennials in autumn or early spring (see Dividing perennials, page 92).

GROWING TIP

Cinquefoils produce long flower stems that can become floppy and need support. Grow them among plants that will provide some structure for the cinquefoil to lean on.

Family Rosaceae	
Height 10–45cm/4–18in	
Spacing 5–7 per m²/ 10 sq. ft	
Flowering time Summer	
Hardiness Zone 7	

Potentilla atrosanguinea

HERALDIC SIGN
The cinquefoil emblem was used in medieval architecture and heraldry to signify power, loyalty and honesty.

Potentilla nepalensis

Primula

Primula aka cowslip, primrose

There are over 500 species of *Primula* and they include the pale yellow common primrose (*P. vulgaris*), the drumstick primula (*P. denticulata*) with its ball of flowers and the tiered blooms of the candelabra primulas. Almost every flower colour can be found in these plants.

—

WHERE TO GROW

Generally, primulas are best grown in a woodland garden or partially shaded border. Some can be planted in the damp soil beside water, including *P. vialii* and the candelabra primulas, like crimson *P. japonica* and orange *P. bulleyana*, while others need better drainage or can be grown in grass.

HOW TO GROW

Most primulas require moist soil so dig in organic matter before planting. The leafy rosettes can be divided in early spring if they have formed a few growing points (see Dividing perennials, page 92), or grow primulas from seed sown in winter (see Growing from seed, page 25).

GROWING TIP

Alpine primulas, like *P. marginata* and *P. auricula*, need good drainage and plenty of light. The exquisite 'show auriculas', bred from *P. auricula*, are traditionally grown in terracotta pots and displayed on shelves in auricula 'theatres'.

Family Primulaceae

Height 10–90cm/ 4–36in

Spacing 7–9 per m²/ 10 sq. ft

Flowering time Late winter–summer

Hardiness Zone 5–7

SCOTTISH JEWEL
The tiny Scottish primrose *P. scotica* grows wild in northern Scotland – and nowhere else.

Primula denticulata

Primula vialii

Lungwort

Pulmonaria

These tough, low-growing plants develop bristly-hairy, often spotted or speckled, oval leaves and short sprays of bell-shaped, blue, pink or white flowers in spring.

—

WHERE TO GROW

Lungwort is a plant for a partially shaded bed or woodland garden, where it can make useful ground cover over the spring and summer. It needs moisture-retentive but not waterlogged soil.

HOW TO GROW

This perennial can cover the ground with its patterned leaves and is often planted more for its foliage than its flowers (see Planting perennials for foliage, page 38). Although an herbaceous perennial, lungwort is often semi-evergreen. New leaves appear with the flowers in early spring. (See also Using perennials in a winter garden, page 46.) Propagate by division in late spring or autumn (see Dividing perennials, page 92).

GROWING TIP

Some cultivars, like *P.* 'Silver Bouquet', have almost entirely silver leaves, and are useful for lighting up a dark corner or awkward shady part of the garden.

Family	Boraginaceae
Height	15–30cm/6–12in
Spacing	7–9 per m²/10 sq. ft
Flowering time	Early spring
Hardiness	Zone 6

Pulmonaria officinalis

BREATHE EASY
Because the spotted leaves look like lungs, they were traditionally used to treat respiratory problems.

Pulmonaria officinalis

Rodgersia
Rodgersia

Wide, exotic-looking, palmate or pinnate, heavily veined leaves on long stems are the prominent features of rodgersia. The tiny flowers are held in densely packed, conical panicles in summer.

—

WHERE TO GROW
Grow in fertile soil and partial shade in a woodland garden or in deep moist soil beside a pond or stream. If the soil retains moisture, rodgersias can be grown in full sun, as well as partial shade, but they can be scorched in hot direct sunlight.

HOW TO GROW
Cut back the leaves of these herbaceous perennials when they die down during autumn. Propagate by division in spring or autumn (see Dividing perennials, page 92).

GROWING TIP
Rodgersias form clumps of slowly spreading rhizomes, which should be lifted and divided in early spring every few years, to regenerate the plant (see Dividing perennials, page 92).

Family Saxifragaceae	
Height 1–1.5m/3–5ft	
Spacing 2–3 per m²/ 10 sq. ft	
Flowering time Mid–late summer	
Hardiness Zone 6	

CHESTNUT-LEAVED
Rodgersia aesculifolia is named after the horse chestnut (*Aesculus*) tree, which its palmate leaves resemble.

Rodgersia aesculifolia

Rodgersia podophylla

Mixing perennials with grasses

Ornamental grasses make wonderful companion plants for border perennials. They bring a different form and texture and can be used as a focal point or as a background to a display of flowers. Grasses range from low and tufted to tall and wispy, so think about how you want to use a grass and choose one that will combine best with your perennials.

In summer, it is the leaves of grasses that are their main feature. Some, like the Magellan rye grass (*Elymus magellanicus*) or blue fescue (*Festuca glauca*), have striking blue leaves. Japanese blood grass (*Imperata cylindrica* 'Rubra') produces leaves stained with red. They contribute to the colour scheme of a border. The fine leaves of prairie dropseed (*Sporobolus heterolepis*) provide a low cover that other plants can grow through, to create a flower-meadow effect.

Late summer and autumn are when ornamental grasses bring something special to a border. The seed heads and the leaves start to brown, sometimes with wonderful autumnal colours. The russet tones are a good match for late perennials, like ice plant (*Hylotelephium*), sneezeweed (*Helenium*) and black-eyed Susan (*Rudbeckia*).

Grasses can form a screen that divides a border or can act as a semi-transparent veil. The feather reed grass (*Calamagrostis* × *acutiflora* 'Karl Foerster') forms tall upright clumps that create a barrier or dense background. Some *Miscanthus* can also be used to enclose a space. Forms of the tall purple moor-grass (*Molinia arundinacea*) are more transparent, allowing flowers to mingle with the grass stems.

The majority of ornamental grasses are herbaceous and need to be cut back in late winter. Don't cut them back too early as you'll miss the frosted seed heads sparkling on a clear winter morning.

A The leaves of Japanese blood grass are stained red in summer.

B Flower spikes of Culver's root (*Veronicastrum virginicum* 'Album') here rise above a frothy cloud of tufted hair grass (*Deschampsia cespitosa* 'Schottland').

C In late summer, *Calamagrostis* × *acutiflora* 'Karl Foerster' creates a golden backdrop to black-eyed Susan, the seed heads of Turkish sage (*Phlomis russeliana*) and autumnal flowers of ice plant.

D *Cenchrus* (syn. *Pennisetum*) *alopecuroides* 'Red Head' forms a focal point in this border, accompanied by the ice plant *Hylotelephium* 'Matrona'.

E Cut grasses back by late winter. Don't shorten to ground level because you could damage any new shoots, which will soon start to grow once temperatures rise.

Black-eyed Susan

Rudbeckia aka coneflower

The sunniest brightest flowers for late summer are provided by perennial rudbeckias, which are reliable plants that have a long flowering season. Their daisy blooms have greenish-yellow to rich golden yellow rays and a black or green cone at the centre.

—

WHERE TO GROW

Plant black-eyed Susan in moisture-retentive but well-drained soil. They will survive, but not thrive, in a drought and are the perfect plant for a sunny herbaceous border. They are also good for naturalistic, prairie-style planting, mixed with grasses (see Mixing perennials with grasses, page 118 and Naturalistic planting, page 17).

HOW TO GROW

Propagation is easy from division in late spring or after flowering (see Dividing perennials, page 92). Black-eyed Susan can also seed around, which can be a problem so weed out any that appear in unwanted locations.

GROWING TIP

If you want to add height to a border, plant cut-leaved coneflower (*R. laciniata*), which can reach up to 2.5m/8ft, so needs support (see Planting tall perennials to add height, page 128). Other rudbeckias are much shorter and in a sunny spot will not need staking.

Family Asteraceae

Height 0.6–2.5m/2–8ft

Spacing 3–7 per m²/ 10 sq. ft

Flowering time Late summer–autumn

Hardiness Zone 6

Rudbeckia hirta var. *pulcherrima*

TEA TONIC
Ground-up petals of black-eyed Susan have been made into tea or soup and also were traditionally given to children with worms.

Rudbeckia hirta

Sage

Salvia aka clary

Salvia is a huge genus with over 1,000 species, including annuals, herbaceous perennials and tender shrubs. All have hooded flowers each with a drooping lower lip, in almost every colour imaginable. The foliage is aromatic.

—

WHERE TO GROW

Most sages need full sun, in an herbaceous border, naturalistic planting, cottage-garden-style planting or dry garden. Some are good in pots. See also Mixing perennials with grasses, page 118; and Repeating plants to unify a border, page 60.

HOW TO GROW

Plant the hardy perennials, like *S. × sylvestris* 'Mainacht' and *S. nemorosa* 'Caradonna', in well-drained, moisture-retentive soil. Some, like *S. yangii* (syn. *Perovskia atriplicifolia*), are drought tolerant. Later-flowering sages include colourful, half-hardy species from Mexico that need a warm location, such as against a sunny wall.

GROWING TIP

Take softwood cuttings in summer, especially from the half-hardy sages like *S. patens* and *S.* 'Amistad', to ensure you have replacement plants after a cold winter (see Taking stem cuttings to get more plants, page 102).

Salvia × sylvestris 'Mainacht'

Family Lamiaceae	
Height 0.3–2m/1–7ft	
Spacing 3–7 per m²/10 sq. ft	
Flowering time Early summer–autumn	
Hardiness Zone 4–6	

COOK IT
Common sage (*S. officinalis*) is among the less pretty species but is a popular culinary herb.

Salvia pratensis

Burnet

Sanguisorba aka pimpernel

These increasingly popular perennials produce
attractive divided foliage and airy sprays of white,
pink or maroon flowers. The tiny individual flowers
are held in compact, cylindrical, oval or rounded,
button-like heads.

—

WHERE TO GROW
Burnet needs full sun to partial shade and well-drained
but moisture-retentive soil. Grow in a sunny herbaceous
border, flower meadow or prairie-style planting,
with grasses (see Mixing perennials with grasses,
page 118).

HOW TO GROW
Taller species of burnet are suitable for a more
informal style of planting, mingling with other
plants. Cut back stems in late winter and divide
the rhizomatous clumps in spring or autumn,
to increase your stock (see Dividing perennials,
page 92).

GROWING TIP
Some taller burnets can produce masses of flower
heads and become top-heavy. Provide support to
prevent them flopping over or grow with upright grasses
that will hold them up.

| Family Rosaceae |
| Height 0.3–2m/1–7ft |
| Spacing 3–5 per m²/ 10 sq. ft |
| Flowering time Mid–late summer |
| Hardiness Zone 7 |

Sanguisorba officinalis

SALAD DAYS
Salad burnet (*S. minor*)
is a European and Asian
wild flower grown for its
leaves, which taste slightly
of cucumber.

*Sanguisorba
officinalis*

Prairie mallow

Sidalcea

Prairie mallow has low tufts of rounded leaves that give rise to tall leafy stems bearing racemes of pale to deep pink or white, mallow-like flowers with silky, sometimes fringed, petals.

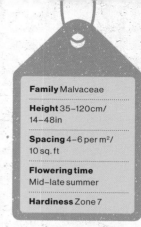

Family Malvaceae	
Height 35–120cm/ 14–48in	
Spacing 4–6 per m²/ 10 sq. ft	
Flowering time Mid–late summer	
Hardiness Zone 7	

WHERE TO GROW

Grow prairie mallow in moist but well-drained soil in full sun or partial shade. Position in an herbaceous border, a cottage-garden-style planting scheme or flower meadow among low grasses (see Mixing perennials with grasses, page 118).

HOW TO GROW

Prairie mallow can flower for several weeks from mid- to late summer. It often doesn't survive in winter if the soil becomes waterlogged. In a garden with heavy soil, it can be short-lived, but you can grow it in a container (see Planting a container with perennials, page 82). Propagate by division in early spring (see Dividing perennials, page 92).

GROWING TIP

Staking is rarely needed, even in forms that reach over 1m/3ft tall, as their stems are strong.

Sidalcea
malviflora

Sidalcea oregana

NAME COMBO
Sidalcea comes from joining the names of two closely related genera, *Sida* and *Alcea* (hollyhock).

Campion

Silene aka *Lychnis,* Jerusalem cross, Maltese cross, rose campion

Campions can be annuals, alpines or herbaceous perennials. Two popular species, previously known as *Lychnis*, are the bright magenta rose campion (*S. coronaria*) and scarlet-red Maltese cross (*S. chalcedonica*).

—

WHERE TO GROW

Most herbaceous perennial campions can be grown in a sunny border in any free-draining soil. Maltese cross likes a little more moisture in the soil but can be grown in the same conditions as other campions, as long as the soil isn't too dry. Small species, like *S. schafta*, make good container plants.

HOW TO GROW

Campions are easy to propagate from seed sown in late winter (see Growing from seed, page 25), or take basal shoot cuttings in early summer (see Stem cuttings, page 27).

GROWING TIP

Rose campion has silvery grey, felted leaves and striking magenta flowers that look best scattered through other plants, to add a contrasting splash of bright colour.

Family Caryophyllaceae	
Height 30–100cm/ 12–39in	
Spacing 5–7 per m²/ 10 sq. ft	
Flowering time Early–midsummer	
Hardiness Zone 7	

Silene coronaria

RED CROSS
Folklore suggests the Maltese cross was brought from Asia to Europe by the Knights of Malta.

Silene chalcedonica

Golden rod

Solidago aka woundwort

Golden rod has a reputation for being invasive, but the smaller, better-behaved varieties make a bright, late summer show, when great fountains of yellow flowers are borne in arching sprays or loose conical heads.

—

WHERE TO GROW

This is an easy plant to grow in a sunny herbaceous border, cottage-garden-style scheme or among grasses in prairie-style planting (see Mixing perennials with grasses, page 118). The soil should be free-draining and doesn't need to be very fertile.

HOW TO GROW

Golden rod often colonizes waste ground, where it gets no attention at all, but it does need plenty of sun to grow well. Look out for less invasive forms and propagate these by division in spring (see Dividing perennials, page 92).

GROWING TIP

Invasive species, like *S. canadensis*, can fill a border if left unchecked. Cut off the flowers once finished, to prevent them spreading their seeds.

Family Asteraceae

Height 0.5–2.5m/ 1½–8ft

Spacing 5–7 per m²/ 10 sq. ft

Flowering time Late summer–autumn

Hardiness Zone 7

BOUNCE BACK
The leaves of golden rod contain about 7 per cent natural rubber.

Solidago canadensis

Solidago canadensis

Meadow rue

Thalictrum

From tufts of ferny glaucous leaves grow medium to tall, upright stems that hold many small flowers with prominent stamens, held in densely packed or open airy panicles.

—

WHERE TO GROW

Meadow rue needs moisture-retentive, fertile soil. Its fluffy clouds of flowers make it suitable for informal planting styles, in naturalistic planting, a cottage-style garden, woodland garden or sunny to partially shaded border.

HOW TO GROW

As meadow rue is not drought tolerant, it survives in full sun only if the soil doesn't dry out. It can be a tall plant so is best grown at the back or middle of a border. Propagate by dividing established clumps in early spring (see Dividing perennials, page 92).

GROWING TIP

Although quite sturdy, the tallest varieties, like the popular *T.* 'Elin', can reach 2.5/8ft and will need support, especially in more exposed positions.

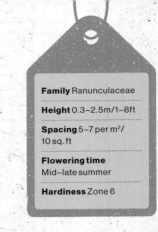

Family Ranunculaceae

Height 0.3–2.5m/1–8ft

Spacing 5–7 per m²/ 10 sq. ft

Flowering time Mid–late summer

Hardiness Zone 6

Thalictrum aquilegiifolium

CHINESE MEDICINE
At least forty-three species of *Thalictrum* are used medicinally in China, for various conditions.

Thalictrum flavum

Globeflower

Trollius

The lemon-yellow flowers of *T. europaeus* have wide sepals that curve inwards, making a rounded shape. Other species have pale yellow to orange, more saucer-shaped blooms, each with a cluster of anthers at the centre.

—

WHERE TO GROW
These are mostly plants of damp places so plant them in deep moist soil in a border, bog garden or alongside a stream or pond.

HOW TO GROW
If the soil remains moist, globeflowers can be grown in full sun or partial shade. They will make a tuft of glossy, deeply lobed leaves that can be divided after flowering. Seed should be sown as fresh as possible, for quick germination (see Growing from seed, page 25).

GROWING TIP
Globeflowers have a short flowering season, finishing by early summer, so you will need to fill the gap for the rest of the summer or else hide the fading globeflowers behind later-flowering plants.

Family Ranunculaceae	
Height 30–90cm/ 12–36in	
Spacing 7–9 per m²/ 10 sq. ft	
Flowering time Late spring–early summer	
Hardiness Zone 6–7	

Trollius europaeus

Trollius europaeus

GOLDEN BALL
The name *Trollius* comes from the Swiss-German *Trollblume*, meaning rounded flower.

Planting tall perennials to add height

Growing tall plants in a border will introduce variety, help screen your garden or hide a building, and can keep the border in scale with surrounding structures. Shrubs or small trees are often used for this, but you should also consider tall perennials. You won't have to worry about pruning them or what they look like in winter. Just cut them down in late autumn and wait for the fresh new growth in spring.

Although herbaceous perennials die down for winter, they often have structural form right through autumn. Some can reach over 2m/7ft and are topped by colourful flowers for several weeks. Most need full sun, to prevent them leaning towards the light, as well as fertile soil to provide the nutrients needed to reach their maximum height.

To hide a building or view, use a stout leafy perennial like Joe Pye weed (*Eutrochium*) or plume poppy (*Macleaya*). They will not conceal a building completely but will break up its outline and soften the view. *Inula magnifica* is a large perennial with wide leaves that will hide a wall. It will also add mass to a planting, easing the transition between low plants at the front of a border and the high wall or hedge behind.

The willow-leaved sunflower (*Helianthus salicifolius*) and cut-leaved coneflower (*Rudbeckia laciniata*) have waving stems that break up a view without obscuring it completely. Tall perennials with a more open habit, like purple top (*Verbena bonariensis*) and giant scabious (*Cephalaria gigantea*), can distract the eye from the scene beyond.

Tall herbaceous perennials may not be a permanent feature, but at the time of year when you are most likely to be sitting in your garden they provide a sense of enclosure and some privacy.

A In this transition from short to tall plants in a border are cranesbill (*Geranium*), then spurge (*Euphorbia wallichii*) while the taller meadowsweet (*Filipendula*) and pale yellow *Thalictrum lucidum* form a backdrop.

B Joe Pye weed (*Eutrochium*), here on the left rising above the white Japanese anemone (*Eriocapitella* 'Honorine Jobert') and Wallich spurge (*Euphorbia wallichii*), can reach over 2m/7ft tall and be used as a summer screen.

C The plume poppy (*Macleaya*) has upright leafy stems topped by the sprays of small beige flowers, which can be planted so it blocks a view.

D Tall perennials like cut-leaved coneflower (*Rudbeckia laciniata*) fill the space between the lower plants at the front of a border and a high wall behind.

E The willow-leaved sunflower (*Helianthus salicifolius*) has yellow blooms on tall stems that can be used to distract the eye. They become more floppy as the season progresses.

Mullein

Verbascum

Many biennials as well as perennial species suitable for gardens are included in this large genus. These mostly have rosettes of hairy leaves and upright flower spikes, with a succession of rounded, outward-facing blooms. Look out for cultivars of perennial species like *V. chaixii* and *V. phoeniceum*.

Family Scrophulariaceae

Height 0.3–2m/1–7ft

Spacing 3–5 per m²/ 10 sq. ft

Flowering time Early–midsummer

Hardiness Zone 6

WHERE TO GROW

Perennial mulleins generally do best in full sun but can grow in partial shade. Grow them in moist, free-draining soil that is never waterlogged in a sunny border or scattered through an informal planting scheme.

HOW TO GROW

Species can be grown from seed, sown in autumn or spring (see Growing from seed, page 25), but they frequently hybridize so propagate cultivars by division or from root cuttings in late winter, to maintain their characteristics (see Dividing perennials, page 92, and Root cuttings, page 28).

GROWING TIP

Perennial mulleins can be short-lived but their lifespan can be extended by cutting back the stems after flowering, leaving the basal rosette of leaves to build up strength.

Verbascum chaixii 'Album'

KEW RAISED
Verbascum 'Helen Johnson' first appeared at the Royal Botanic Gardens, Kew, and was named after one of Kew's gardeners.

Verbascum phoeniceum

Vervain

Verbena aka purple top

Almost ubiquitous in contemporary planting schemes is purple top (*V. bonariensis*), which has tight heads of purple flowers on tall, slender, branching stems. Other hardy perennial vervains, like *V. hastata* and common verbena (*V. officinalis*), have thin spikes of small flowers.

—

WHERE TO GROW

Most vervains like a hot sunny location and free-draining soil. Grow in an informal herbaceous border, a gravel garden (see Making a gravel garden, page 68) or among grasses in prairie-style planting (see Mixing perennials with grasses, page 118). See also Planting tall perennials to add height, page 128.

HOW TO GROW

Vervains often self-seed prolifically and look best when mixed with other plants and free to spread themselves around. They can take over so be vigilant in thinning out self-seeded plants. Sowing seed in spring is the easiest way to propagate them (see Growing from seed, page 25).

GROWING TIP

Plants like purple top are known as 'transparents', because you can readily see through the stems to other plants behind, while still bringing colour and presence to a border.

Verbena bonariensis

Family Verbenaceae	
Height 0.6–2m/2–7ft	
Spacing 5–7 per m²/ 10 sq. ft	
Flowering time Early–late summer	
Hardiness Zone 4–5	

HOLY HERB
Common verbena is a sacred herb used in religious ceremonies since the Roman Empire.

Verbena officinalis

Speedwell

Veronica

This is a very diverse group of plants, from ground-hugging mats to tall border perennials. Each flower, held on a raceme, is commonly blue, lilac or purple, with four petals and two protruding stamens.

—

WHERE TO GROW

Most speedwells can be grown in full sun or partial shade, in soil that remains moist in summer but isn't waterlogged. Some low-growing species, like *V. prostrata*, need good drainage. Plant low forms at the front of a border or raised bed. The taller herbaceous species, like *V. longifolia*, can be grown in a sunny border or cottage-garden-style planting scheme.

HOW TO GROW

Propagate herbaceous species by division in autumn (see Dividing perennials, page 92) or softwood cuttings of dwarf forms in summer (see Taking stem cuttings to get more plants, page 102).

GROWING TIP

Brooklime (*V. beccabunga*) is a creeping marginal aquatic that needs wet soil by a pond, or it can be planted in shallow water.

Family Plantaginaceae

Height 20–120cm/ 8–48in

Spacing 5–7 per m²/ 10 sq. ft

Flowering time Spring–midsummer

Hardiness Zone 7

Veronica prostrata

KIWI CLAN
The shrubby hebes from New Zealand are now included in the genus *Veronica*.

Veronica longifolia

Culver's root

Veronicastrum aka Black root

North American Culver's root (*V. virginicum*) and its cultivars are tall herbaceous perennials with attractive leafy stems and slender spires of densely packed flowers. Asian *V. sibiricum* is similar but less often grown in gardens.

—

WHERE TO GROW

Plant in moisture-retentive, free-draining soil, in full sun or partial shade. It is not very drought tolerant, but you should avoid planting in waterlogged ground.

HOW TO GROW

Culver's root can reach 2m/7ft tall so position near the back of a border, where it provides a strong vertical form. Divide established clumps in spring, as the stems emerge, or after cutting back in autumn (see Dividing perennials, page 92).

GROWING TIP

These upright plants don't usually need staking, although support will be necessary in exposed locations.

Family	Plantaginaceae
Height	1.25–2m/4–7ft
Spacing	4–6 per m²/10 sq. ft
Flowering time	Early–midsummer
Hardiness	Zone 7

FASCINATING

Veronicastrum is prone to fasciation, which deforms the flower spikes, particularly in the cultivar *V. virginicum* 'Fascination'.

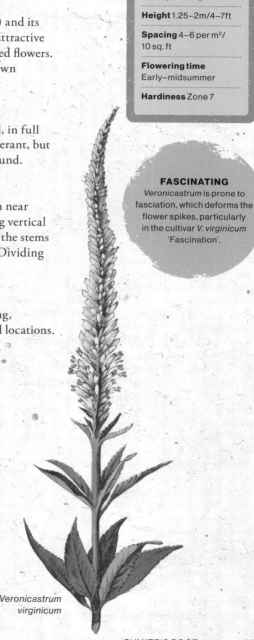

Veronicastrum virginicum

Veronicastrum virginicum

Troubleshooting

LIVING WITH BIODIVERSITY

The group of plants commonly referred to as perennials is extremely diverse, so it is no surprise that they are susceptible to most common pests and diseases. Some are specific to a particular plant, like lupin aphid, while others, like powdery mildew, can be found across many different plants. If you grow perennials in your garden, at some point they will be attacked by something that wants to eat them or colonize them. The most important advice is to not panic.

Fungi, insects and other invertebrates are all part of a functioning healthy ecosystem, along with all living things, including plants, animals and birds. Biodiversity should be encouraged. A functioning ecosystem carries out vital services, such as pollinating plants, cleansing water and decomposing waste. We might not realize the importance of biodiversity until it's irreparably degraded, but that is happening now. For example, there has been an alarming drop in insect numbers over the last few decades. Worldwide, more than 40 per cent of insects are declining and a third are endangered. In the UK, the population of flying insects has declined by 60 per cent in the last twenty years. This is mainly due to pesticide use, rising temperatures and habitat destruction and fragmentation.

So, when faced with a plant in your garden being eaten by a colony of insects, what do you do? You can spray with a poisonous chemical to kill them. You can spray with a less poisonous, and therefore less effective, substance to kill or deter some of them. You can ignore them and let nature take its course, or you can change the way you grow your plants, to try and make your garden more resilient to pest outbreaks.

A commercial grower may have to resort to the first option. Their livelihood may depend on a good crop of plants. For the rest of us, the last option is the one we should be pursuing. As gardeners, we have the power to make changes, to help maintain and boost biodiversity. Our gardens are habitats, even if only on a small scale. If we all have a go at encouraging biodiversity, the difference could be significant.

CULTIVATION AND PHYSICAL TECHNIQUES

Cultivation techniques for pest control are methods that aim to provide the best conditions for growing plants. Plants that are healthy and vigorous are better able to resist a pest attack. They won't be immune, but they should recover from damage more quickly than a plant that is weak

Biodiversity should be protected and encouraged. The wildlife in your garden, like this small copper butterfly, is part of a healthy functioning ecosystem.

Remove leaves that are being eaten by caterpillars, to stop them spreading. Early action is vital to prevent infestations getting out of control.

Fungal diseases, like mildew (top) and rust (bottom), can look unsightly but don't usually kill vigorous plants. Don't put infected plants in your compost as the spores can survive over winter.

or stressed. Choose plants that are adapted to the type of conditions in your garden. If your garden is sunny and has light, free-draining soil, use drought-tolerant plants. If it is cool and shady, plant woodland species. Stress from lack of water can cause weak slow growth that is more susceptible to insect attacks.

Growing a diverse range of plants can reduce the likelihood that your border will be ruined by a single type of pest. Your garden is more likely to be laid to waste by environmental conditions, such as a long drought. Too little water will severely damage plants, while hot sun can scorch the leaves of plants used to partial shade.

Conversely, waterlogged soil can cause many plants to rot at the base. Therefore, pay attention to your plants' needs; you are then more than halfway to maintaining a healthy garden.

There are, of course, pests that feed on the healthiest plants and, if left to get out of control, can severely damage or kill them. The most common are insects that feed on the sap in juicy leaves and stems, such as aphids (also called greenfly or blackfly). They can cause distorted growth and aborted flowers. This weakens the plant and leaves it vulnerable to fungal infections, as well as looking unsightly. Other insects or their larvae feed on the leaves themselves and, in the worst cases, can completely defoliate a plant.

Early observation of any pest or disease can ensure timely action to prevent its spread. For example, squashing aphids between your fingers as soon as you've seen them can slow any invasion. Cutting off any infected shoots will help, as will removing leaves that are being eaten by caterpillars. Picking off slugs and snails when you first see leaf damage will delay their progress. None of these techniques will solve the problem completely, and sometimes you just have to reconsider what plants you are growing. If your lupins are destroyed by lupin aphid every year, then think about growing something else. You can also learn to tolerate some level of damage and think of ways to hide it. Some plants are susceptible to powdery mildew, but it doesn't necessarily kill them, so plant something in front to hide the grey, dusty-looking foliage and you can still enjoy the flowers held above them.

Soil is the most important part of any garden, so look after it (see Improving the soil, page 21). Regular digging will destroy the structure of your soil and damage the underground ecosystem that is so important for soil health. Digging also brings up weed seeds that will then germinate. Healthy soil is a vital part of a balanced ecosystem. It is home to beneficial insects and provides the nutrients plants need. Adding soil improver, such as garden compost or leafmould (see Making your own mulch, page 52), to a new border will generate a good soil structure and help retain moisture, but once the border is planted try and avoid unnecessary digging. Instead, mulch the soil every year to provide nutrients (see Mulching, page 22). If a plant is not flowering well or has formed a clump that is dying in the centre, then you can dig it up and divide it to reinvigorate growth (see Dividing perennials, page 92), but there is no need to dig the whole border. Restrict any digging to what is required to maintain healthy plants.

THE LAST RESORT

If a pest is getting out of control, and physical and cultivation techniques are not enough, then you may have to resort to another treatment. You can spray aphids with soapy water, which blocks their breathing pores and kills them, but this can also damage the waxy cuticle of the plant's leaves if used too often or if the solution is too strong, so introduce it sparingly. Some sprays deter rather than kill pests. For example, garlic spray can discourage some beetles and larvae. Chilli powder can be used to put off squirrels, while pheromones can disrupt insect reproduction and so control populations.

More potent pesticides are available for gardeners and, although they may kill a pest in the short term, there are significant disadvantages to using them. Residues from chemical sprays collect in the soil and make their way to ponds and streams, eventually ending up in the water we drink and the food we eat. Insecticides can kill everything, including the bees that pollinate the flowers, the parasitic wasps that prey on whitefly, and ladybirds, whose larvae eat aphids. You will be killing these beneficial insects as well as the pest you are trying to eradicate. Therefore, think twice before applying chemical sprays. A garden should be a haven for wildlife, as well as a beautiful place for us to enjoy.

What to do when

WINTER

In winter, the garden is resting and most perennials are dormant. This is the time to tidy up your borders in preparation for the year ahead.

- Cut back any remaining old stems and foliage from the previous year's perennials, being careful not to damage new shoots that will start to grow by the end of winter.
- When cutting back plants, try not to tread on emerging winter bulbs like snowdrops (*Galanthus*), winter aconites (*Eranthis*) or early crocus.
- If you are growing ornamental grasses with your perennials, now is the time to cut them back (see Mixing perennials with grasses, page 118).
- Put old stems and leaves on a compost heap so they can rot down and create mulch for your garden (see Making your own mulch, page 52).
- In early winter and provided the ground isn't frozen, use compost made the previous year to mulch any parts of the garden you didn't get around to in autumn (see Mulching, page 22).
- There won't be many weeds at this time of year but if you remove any you see now it will save more weeding later in the year.
- Cut off the old leaves of hellebores (*Helleborus*) just as the flower buds begin to emerge. This removes diseased foliage and makes room for the new leaves and flowers (see Using perennials in a winter garden, page 46).
- Divide perennials while they are dormant. Dig them up, split the clumps and replant them straight away (see Dividing perennials, page 92).
- In late winter, sow seeds you have collected from your garden (see Growing from seed, page 25). There is time for them to have a few weeks of cold weather, which is often needed to start germination. Protect the pots from wind and rain.
- If temperatures of more than a few degrees below freezing are forecast, move any pots of perennials to a sheltered position to prevent them freezing solid.

SPRING

As spring progresses so does the growth of perennials. Change is rapid by late spring, so make sure you leave some time to enjoy the garden.

- Spring is a good time to plant perennials (see Planting and aftercare, page 20). The soil is warming up and the days are long so they will get a good start. Remember to plant in groups instead of single plants, and if you can repeat some plants – it will help the

Winter and early spring are good times to tidy your border. Remove weeds as they start to grow, and cut back old growth on perennials as the new shoots start to emerge.

border look more coherent (see Repeating plants to unify a border, page 60).

- Cut back evergreen perennials and subshrubs you have left over winter, like penstemons. This will stimulate new growth from the base.
- As perennials start to grow, think about which ones will need staking (see Support your plants, page 23). Make a frame around and over each plant with sticks, canes or ready-made plant supports, to stop the stems falling over in summer.
- Seed sown in winter will start to germinate. Prick out the seedlings into individual pots to grow on.
- Collect seed of winter- or early spring-flowering plants. It is important to sow

hellebore seeds straight away, while they are still fresh.

- As perennials start to grow, so will weeds so make sure you remove weed seedlings as they appear.
- Start to look out for pests like aphids (see Cultivation and physical techniques, page 136). Catching them early and removing them will help to control pest populations before they take over.

SUMMER

Summer is the peak season for most perennials. It's when they reach their maximum size and can flower for several weeks.

Planting in autumn gives new plants a good start, as the soil is still warm. Roots will grow before winter, and the plants will be ready to flourish once spring arrives.

- Remove faded flowers (deadhead) to encourage more flowers to open.
- Trim back early summer perennials, including cranesbill (*Geranium*) like G. 'Orion' and G. 'Brookside' and sages (*Salvia*) like S. × *sylvestris* 'Serenade' and S. × s. 'Mainacht', quite hard after flowering. This often results in a second flush of bloom later in summer.
- Keep a check on moisture in the soil, and water plants if it becomes dry. Do not overwater, as this can cause plants to form surface roots only, making them less likely to survive a dry spell.
- Give perennials in pots more water, as the soil can dry out quickly. During a spell of hot dry weather, containers may

need watering every day.
- Provide some support for any plant that is starting to collapse under the weight of its flowers, if you didn't stake it earlier in the year (see Support your plants, page 23). Push sticks or canes into the ground around the plant, to try and hold up the stems.
- Keep checking for pests and diseases as they could be taking over by now (see Cultivation and physical techniques, page 136). Remove damaged or infected plant material. Material damaged by insects can be put on the compost heap, as the pests will quickly die once the plant begins to decay.
- Carry on weeding. Look out for weeds

that are about to set seed. Catching them before they disperse their seeds will save a lot of weeding next year.

- From early summer, take softwood cuttings of plants you want to propagate. Look for strong, healthy, non-flowering shoots (see Taking stem cuttings to get more plants, page 102). Cuttings can be rooted all through summer if there is good material.
- Visit other gardens for ideas and inspiration. You might see a plant you didn't know or a combination you hadn't thought of, so make notes or take photographs.
- Look through your border for any gaps that need filling or plants that don't work well together. Make a note of changes to do once summer is over.

AUTUMN

Autumn is the best season to plant (see Planting and aftercare, page 20). The soil is still warm from the summer sun, and new plants will start growing roots before winter.

- Before planting, clear the area of weeds and cut back perennials that are remaining, to give yourself room to get in and plant.
- Visit gardens to see late-flowering perennials and note colours that look good alongside the autumn foliage of trees and shrubs.
- Collect seed of late spring- and summer-flowering perennials if you want to try growing them from seed. Collect the seed heads in a paper bag and leave them to dry out (see Growing from seed, page 25).
- Leave plants for wildlife when they have finished flowering. The dry stems and foliage can still add interest to

a border and the seeds are food for animals and birds (see Delay cutting back perennials, page 108).

- Cut back stems and leaves when they become too untidy or collapse completely. Put them on the compost heap.
- Remove dead and damaged leaves from evergreen perennials.
- Do not cut back subshrubs, like penstemons or sages (*Salvia*) such as *S. greggii* and *S. × jamensis*, as this will cause them to die if there is a very cold spell. Wait until spring.
- Collect fallen leaves of deciduous trees to make leafmould. Pile them in a wire cage or plastic bin liner so they rot down, ready to use in a year or two (see Making your own mulch, page 52).
- Once you have cut back your perennials, mulch the soil in late autumn as long as the ground isn't frozen (see Mulching, page 22).
- Make sure any cold-sensitive plants are protected before the first frosts occur. Bring them into a greenhouse, conservatory or porch, or cover with horticultural fleece.
- Divide perennials now in areas that have very cold winters, rather than in winter.

Index

Quarto

First published in 2023 by Frances Lincoln,
an imprint of Quarto.
One Triptych Place,
London, SE1 9SH
United Kingdom
T (0)20 7700 6700 F (0)20 7700 8066
www.Quarto.com

A catalogue record for this book is available from the
British Library.

ISBN 978-0-7112-8243-8
eISBN 978-0-7112-8244-5

10 9 8 7 6 5 4 3 2 1

Typeset in Adobe Garamond and
Neue Haas Grotesk Display
Design by Arianna Osti

Printed in China

Photographic acknowledgments

GAP Photos: 29

Richard Wilford: 12, 14, 18 left + right, 21 left + right, 23, 27, 33, 35, 39, 42, 47, 53, 61, 69, 70, 72, 75, 83, 93, 95, 97, 103, 105, 106, 109, 119, 129, 131, 132, 135, 140

Shutterstock: 2 (Gardens by Design), 6–7 (Galina Bolshakova 69), 9 (cornfield), 10 (Stanley Dullea), 13 (Andrew Fletcher), 15 (Molly Shannon), 16 (Peter Turner Photography), 22 (Beekeepx), 24 (Zsolyomi), 25 (KAMONRAT), 26 (Max_555), 30–1 (MalcolmC), 32 (tamu1500), 34 (Josie Elias), 36 (Danny Hummel), 37 (Jana Loesch), 40 (Nahhana), 41 (Ole Schoener), 43 (znmysteryPhoto), 44 (Alex Manders), 45 (Ken Schulze), 49 (Iva Vagnerova), 50 (LapailrKrapai), 51 (photoPOU), 54 (guentermanaus), 55 (Golden Shark 2), 56 (Ilona5555), 57 (Iryna Imago), 58 (Akif CUBUK), 59 (Alex Manders), 62 (Alex Manders), 63 (Beekeepx), 64 (John R. Martin), 65 (SimoneHa), 66 (nnattalli), 67 (AngieC333), 71 Barbara Smits, 73 (Alex Manders), 76 (liu yu shan), 77 (Alex Manders), 78 (Flower_Garden), 79 (Natalia van D), 80 (Stampf), 81 (demamiel62), 84 (Leene), 85 (olko1975), 86 (Peter_Fleming), 87 (Ruth Peterkin), 88 (Ingrid Maasik), 89 (Alex Manders), 90 (Krzysztof Slusarczyk), 91 (H. Tanaka), 94 (Ingrid Maasik), 96 (Mariola Anna S), 98 (Anna Gratys), 99 (Doikanoy), 100 (agatchen), 101 (COULANGES), 104 (Birute Vijeikiene), 107 (Alex Manders), 110 (LianeM), 111 (Lacey Dent), 112 (weha), 113 (Natalia Sidorova), 114 (Martin Fowler), 115 (LapailrKrapai), 116 (Anna50), 117 (agatchen), 120 (NataliSel), 121 (Elena Rostunova), 122 (Nick 1), 123 (Manfred Ruckszio), 124 (Emilio100), 125 Victoria Tucholka, 126 (Elena Koromyslova), 127 (Cristian Gusa), 130 (Alex Manders), 133 (LapailrKrapai), 136 left (RJ22), 136 right above (HelloSSTK), 136 right below (Maryna Zhukova), 139 (Marina.Martinez)